W0091389

SAGE was founded in 1965 by Sara Miller McCune to support the dissemination of usable knowledge by publishing innovative and high-quality research and teaching content. Today, we publish over 900 journals, including those of more than 400 learned societies, more than 800 new books per year, and a growing range of library products including archives, data, case studies, reports, and video. SAGE remains majority-owned by our founder, and after Sara's lifetime will become owned by a charitable trust that secures our continued independence.

Los Angeles | London | New Delhi | Singapore | Washington DC | Melbourne

Advance Praise

The authors of *The VUCA Company* have advanced the scholarly contribution with its sequel, *The VUCA Learner*. They have tried to express how in a VUCA world the learner must be prepared to unlearn and then relearn in order to counter the unexpected and unknown. This text is a must-read for all those preparing for a leadership role.

David Ahlstrom, *Professor, Department of Management,*
The Chinese University of Hong Kong;
Senior Editor, Journal of World Business

In a truly turbulent and unpredictable (VUCA) world, this book identifies what it will take to produce learners who are sufficiently able to dive into experience with others without fear, fully engage, step back and learn from their experiences—yet be ready to relearn again and again. Since students both desire this and are scared to death of it, it is a monumental undertaking but totally necessary for economic and societal survival.

Allan R. Cohen, *Distinguished Professor of Global Leadership,*
Babson College, Massachusetts;
Co-author, Influence Without Authority

There may be no more important issue facing labour markets than helping people be more adaptable in their work and careers. Markets are more competitive and rapidly evolving than in the past. Careers are less likely to be along defined paths within a single company. Artificial intelligence is changing jobs in dramatic ways. More skilled jobs are being automated than ever before. To stay ahead, we need to invest in the cognitive, social and innovation skills that distinguish humans from machines. This book comes at exactly the right time, with exactly the right topic. Good luck with your new book.

Michael Gibbs, *Clinical Professor of Economics,*
University of Chicago Booth School of Business Research;
Fellow, IZA-Institute of Labor Economics

The *VUCA Company* provided insights on the failures in a VUCA world. The same authors, in their sequel, *The VUCA Learner*, have expanded their research and insights into how learners should react in unexpected and unknown scenarios. Leaders, working in a networked digital world, will find this book useful and inspiring, which will help them survive and prosper in a VUCA world.

Graham Kendall, *Provost and CEO, and Professor of Computer Science, University of Nottingham Malaysia Campus; Pro Vice Chancellor, University of Nottingham*

A wonderful little book, full of inspiring insights.

Gerard McElwee, *Professor of Entrepreneurship, Huddersfield Business School, University of Huddersfield; Editor, International Journal of Entrepreneurship and Innovation*

The *VUCA Learner* is an interesting book which brings new insights into mechanisms of learning in a VUCA world. I would strongly recommend this book to anyone who may need not only inspiration but also very useful tips about how to become a VUCA learner.

Aidin Salamzadeh, *Editor-in-Chief, Journal of Entrepreneurship, Business and Economics*

VUCA describes perfectly what is happening in the global business world today. Observation, absorption, self-validation combined with selective application are the tools for individuals to swim in this ocean of digital networks.

Nalin Jain, *Senior Consultant–SME, Innovation and Entrepreneurship Trade and Competitiveness, World Bank*

Reading this book would be must for practitioners, academicians and researchers who deal with uncertainty of ever-changing context of business. Delighted to go through it.

Pankaj Kumar, *Professor of Human Resource Management and Organizational Behaviour, Indian Institute of Management Lucknow*

Thinking outside the box to solve problems of today and yet imagining an innovation-filled bright future. In this sequel to their *VUCA Company,* Suhayl Abidi and Manoj Joshi enrich the readers with their wisdom, intellect, analytic rigour and pragmatism.

Tojo Thatchenkery, *Professor and Director, Schar School of Policy and Government, George Mason University, Virginia; Co-author, Appreciative Intelligence: Seeing the Mighty Oak in the Acorn*

The *VUCA Learner* provides considerable insight into learning and the demands placed on the learning in the continuing rise of the knowledge age where the individual must excel at continuous learning.

Roger R. Stough, *University Professor, Schar School of Policy and Government, George Mason University*

The
VUCA
LEARNER

The *VUCA LEARNER*

Future-proof Your Relevance

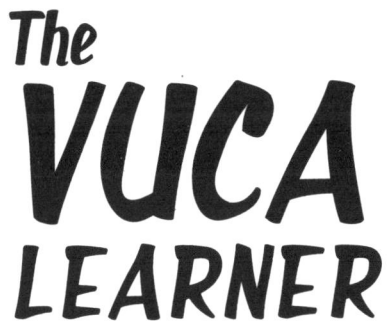

SUHAYL ABIDI
MANOJ JOSHI

Los Angeles | London | New Delhi
Singapore | Washington DC | Melbourne

First published in 2018 by

SAGE Publications India Pvt Ltd
B1/I-1 Mohan Cooperative Industrial Area
Mathura Road, New Delhi 110 044, India
www.sagepub.in

SAGE Publications Inc
2455 Teller Road
Thousand Oaks, California 91320, USA

SAGE Publications Ltd
1 Oliver's Yard, 55 City Road
London EC1Y 1SP, United Kingdom

SAGE Publications Asia-Pacific Pte Ltd
3 Church Street
#10-04 Samsung Hub
Singapore 049483

Published by Vivek Mehra for SAGE Publications India Pvt Ltd, typeset in 13/16 pts Adobe Garamond Pro by Fidus Design Pvt. Ltd., Chandigarh and printed at Chaman Enterprises, New Delhi.

Library of Congress Cataloging-in-Publication Data
Names: Abidi, Suhayl, author. | Joshi, Manoj, author.
Title: The VUCA learner: future-proof your relevance / Suhayl Abidi and Manoj Joshi.
Description: New Delhi, India: SAGE Publications India, 2018. | Includes bibliographical references.
Identifiers: LCCN 2018022458 (print) | LCCN 2018024200 (ebook) | ISBN 9789352807536
     (Web PDF) | ISBN 9789352807529 (E Pub 2.0) | ISBN 9789352807512 (pbk.: alk. paper)
Subjects: LCSH: Organizational learning. | Employees—Training of. | Knowledge management. |
     Organizational change.
Classification: LCC HD58.82 (ebook) | LCC HD58.82 .A3135 2018 (print) | DDC 650.1/3—dc23
LC record available at https://lccn.loc.gov/2018022458

ISBN: 978-93-528-0751-2 (PB)

SAGE Team: Manisha Mathews, Sandhya Gola, Madhurima Thapa and Rajinder Kaur

Dedicated to our parents

Thank you for choosing a SAGE product!
If you have any comment, observation or feedback,
I would like to personally hear from you.

Please write to me at **contactceo@sagepub.in**

Vivek Mehra, Managing Director and CEO, SAGE India.

Bulk Sales

SAGE India offers special discounts
for purchase of books in bulk.
We also make available special imprints
and excerpts from our books on demand.

For orders and enquiries, write to us at

Marketing Department
SAGE Publications India Pvt Ltd
B1/I-1, Mohan Cooperative Industrial Area
Mathura Road, Post Bag 7
New Delhi 110044, India

E-mail us at **marketing@sagepub.in**

Get to know more about SAGE

Be invited to SAGE events, get on our mailing list.
Write today to **marketing@sagepub.in**

This book is also available as an e-book.

A successful career will no longer be about promotion. It will be about mastery.

—Michael Hammer,
Author of *Reengineering the Corporation*

Contents

Foreword by Marshall Goldsmith   xi
Preface   xiii

Chapter 1   Introduction: Why Learn   1
Chapter 2   An Unexpected Learner   21
Chapter 3   The Future of Work: The New
             Workplace   39
Chapter 4   Who Will Win: Preparing for
             the Future   80
Chapter 5   I Am My Own Teacher   105
Chapter 6   The World Is Your Classroom:
             Self-learning Tools   140
Chapter 7   Together We Learn; Together
             We Grow   154
Chapter 8   Family Firm Scion: Learning
             in the Family Business   169
Chapter 9   Hierarchy or Wirearchy: Learning
             in Enterprises   191
Chapter 10   The Road Less Travelled: Learning
             in Entrepreneurship   214
Chapter 11   Future-ready   229

Annexure: Personal SWOT Analysis   241
About the Authors   246

Foreword

The VUCA Learner explores the opportunities of VUCA versus the threats. VUCA, understood in business to stand for volatile, uncertain, complex and ambiguous, takes on a different and far more positive meaning in this book. Here, VUCA stands for vision, understanding, clarity and agility.

With its focus on today's rapid pace of change as the 'new normal', *The VUCA Learner* defines new needs for organizations. For instance, companies no longer need lifelong workers as they did in past generations. Today's agile organizations need versatile and specialized mid- and short-term talent. This is a significant shift from the workplace of the past and requires leaders who can assess and define what the company needs right now rather than what it may need decades from now.

VUCA leaders and learners must be facilitators, unlike in the past when leadership was largely considered to be a top-down function. Leaders were masters of their crafts that doled out their knowledge over time to eager apprentices aspiring to gain wisdom. Today, we have the 'knowledge worker', those mid- and short-term workers who are called into projects because they know far more about what they are doing and what is needed than their boss does.

Fundamentally, the ever-increasing presence of the knowledge worker threatens to render our traditional assumptions about top-down leadership obsolete. It also presents challenges to modern-day leaders that their counterparts in years gone by were not called to address.

This is where you will find *The VUCA Learner* to be most helpful. Learn how you can help your team members, organization and leaders achieve their goals when you yourself are not the expert!

Life is good.

Marshall Goldsmith
International best-selling author/editor of
36 books including *What Got You Here Won't Get You There* and *Triggers*

Preface

The bad news started appearing about two years back, and that was after years of high number of entry-level jobs in the Indian IT industry; the pace is slowing down and in fact, the companies of many shades and kind are shedding jobs, both blue and white collar. This was followed by more bad news by surveys and reports that our education system and re-skilling programmes had started failing. This continuous pessimistic news drove out the good news that many new career opportunities were opening up. In our opinion, a person retiring in about 30 years from now will frequently change jobs, some of which have not yet been invented. In addition, today, there are more opportunities opening up for those who want to venture out on their own.

These changes are a consequence of the fast and constantly changing world that was given an acronym VUCA, which stands for volatile, uncertain, complex and ambiguous. We can either fear this world and get panicky or take this turbulence of unknowns, as a challenge to anticipate, learn and strive in making a better life for ourselves, our families and the world we live in. One thing is certain that we will never see status quo. In this world, we are either going up or down, these fluctuations will never stand still. For those who are alert to the changing environment, the world offers a limitless resource to engage, stimulate and cultivate the imagination. In a networked world, information is always available and shall get easier to access. Insight, and what you actually do with that information, will be the new challenge. In the past, leaders did the thinking and others executed. In future, a VUCA executive will be a thinker as well as a person of action and interest.

Our education system has made us a prisoner of antiquated curriculum and teaching styles. Organized training is not keeping pace with the demands of the workplace. Competency and skills enhancement is not enough, these may get obsolete fast. What is the way out for an executive or even a professional to remain relevant to workplace demands of the present as well as prepare for the future? How should he scan the horizon for new opportunities as well as threats? How should he conduct skills gap analysis? What behavioural changes are required to do all that? There is a continuous unending curiosity!

The answer is clear. Transform yourselves into your own teachers, taking full command of your own learning and career development. The skills for the future are not taught but can be learnt on our own too.

Essentially, what this means is that as the world grows more complicated, more complex and more fluid, opportunities for innovation, imagination and play increase. Information and knowledge begin to function like a currency: the more of it you have, the more opportunities you will have to do things. To stay relevant and grow in this unforgiving business environment, one needs to develop a learning mindset, where continuous lifelong learning becomes a daily habit, to let go of the old and become agile, adaptable and resilient. Else, the rapid change tornadoes around will be merciless! Choose your future, now!

A continuous learner, in whichever profession one is working, is engaged in seamless learning from all stimuli, printed and digital, cloud, social media, experience, peer, mentor, network, etc. The world is changing faster than ever and our skill sets have a shorter and shorter life. Formal training and development efforts must be supplemented by informal learning enabling the person not only to cope with today's challenges but also in learning to anticipate and welcome change.

This capacity for independent learning is essential to each individual's future well-being. Since they are likely to have multiple careers, they will need to continually learn new skills, which are not taught in our institutions. These challenges require that we re-conceptualize parts of our educational system and at the same time find ways to reinforce learning outside of formal education, training and development.

Organizations are only as good as the people who work there, the people who make the brand what it is. To get—and stay—ahead of the competition, it is critical to put yesterday's 'wins' aside and focus on winning today. Striving for constant and never-ending improvement should be the endeavour of every organization.

During our interactions with students, entrepreneurs and professionals, we find an ignorance of the world of learning opportunities, which surrounds them, much of it free of cost. Our smartphones alone can open and widen the scope of anytime–anywhere learning. Eighty per cent of all learning takes place in the informal space. A new culture of learning needs to leverage social and technical infrastructures in new ways.

We decided to initiate research on this curiosity and write this book with two objectives: first, not to fear the future, the contours of which are not clearly visible but view it through the eyes of an explorer, a discoverer of new world, and second, to showcase the various sources and methods for self-learning. Whether you are a novice or a CEO, you must develop the learner mindset, scan the business environment for green shoots of opportunities, regularly conduct a skills gap analysis and use all the tools available to continuously reinvent yourself to be ready for new careers. The world is yours, come forward, explore, learn and keep advancing.

Good luck!

Acknowledgements

We are indebted to our wives, Naheed and Bhoomija, and children Sumaira and Katyayni for patiently bearing with us while occasionally advising on the subject matter. Also thanks to Aarushi, Paarth and Siddharth, the kids who pushed our thinking on becoming a self-learner.

We are also indebted to our friend of many decades Sudhir Bansal who brought us together and has offered us valuable advice on publishing matters. Heartfelt thanks to Dr Aseem Chauhan, Chancellor Amity University, for stimulating intellectual discussions and persuasion to do a sequel on VUCA.

This work would not be in such great shape without the deep knowledge and efforts of our editor at SAGE Publications, Manisha Mathews, and her dedicated team.

Chapter 1
Introduction: Why Learn

The grass is greener where you water it.

—Neil Barringham

The business landscape is changing incredibly fast due to several, often interrelated, factors, such as globalization, disruptive technologies and business models, innovation, flatter and leaner organizations, mergers and acquisitions, restructuring, spin-offs, marketplace disruptions, etc. This rapidly changing business environment is often referred to as VUCA (volatile, uncertain, complex and ambiguous). VUCA best describes the volatile and chaotic business, economic and physical environment that we all now face and must learn how to manage under. There are uncertainties and unknowns that plague decisions as an outcome of an imperfect understanding of complex and ambiguous scenarios. It is not as simple as stated, since each degree of correlation and causality between the variables leads to a complex web for arriving at a decision. Events and actions are often interconnected. If something occurs at one level while affecting individuals and companies, it leads to deeper repercussions on the rest. There is a chain, interdependent or interconnected effect. Yet we must appreciate that the only constant is change and that it cannot be ignored.

Many organizations see VUCA as a threat to their existence but it is also an opportunity if one looks at it as vision, understanding, clarity and agility [1]. Moreover, for all the different types and nature of risks on which we can plan for, it is those where we cannot prepare and anticipate which lead to the most damage. This is where we term the onslaught of unexpected and unknowns. This is what is happening to our education system today, not only in India but also throughout the world. The unexpected and unknowns, and their impacts, cannot be anticipated. Thus, alongside identifying, quantifying and then mitigating, we should embrace the idea that not all change can be clearly foreseen and hence planned. How much foresight and scenario planning can mitigate remains an interesting query. 'This implies that we should inculcate within our families, organizations and states, the power of resilience and the tools required to act effectively in times of crisis thereby minimizing the potentially damaging impact of unexpected change' [2], that is, preparing for the 'unknown unknowns'.

Eminent HR thought leader Dr John Sullivan says,

> The era of long-lasting competencies is gone, and I am predicting that it will never return. Chaos and rapid change are the new norm and will be for decades to come. In the chaotic environment that is today, one thing is clear: the approaches developed for organizing labour and accomplishing work in the industrial era have become barriers to productivity today. No longer do organizations need indefinite access to narrowly skilled talent; instead, they need medium-term access to versatile talent and short-term access to specialized talent. [3]

In a VUCA environment, disruption is the order of the day. The velocity of change is simply staggering. By disruptions, we imply the creation of new order in products, markets and customers. Today's organizations should be nimble, constantly embracing change and correctly aligning their people to critical business strategies. The leadership must stay open-minded to all possibilities and not let the fear of failure prevent them from testing new waters. This is essential to cultivate innovation throughout the business and challenge the way the organization works before or in line with external disruptive forces. Each leader must possess humility and the art of listening to lead this inevitable change as an outcome of VUCA.

Lifelong learning is the very first initial step in becoming an outstanding performer. In today's fast-paced world, if one does not keep shedding the old knowledge and embrace new learning, one is not standing still but is falling behind. The pace of learning and acquiring newer knowledge must keep pace with time and, at the same time, unlearning must speed up, implying stale knowledge must be shredded off with time. Mahatma Gandhi said, 'Live as if you were to die tomorrow. Learn as if you were to live forever.'

Today, most CEOs' concern is to develop agile and resilient employees. Agility in an individual can be described as a presence of curiosity to get to the root causes, having a broad perspective, having the ability to find parallels and contrasts, questioning conventional wisdom and finding solutions to tough problems. It is also about the choices they make and the trade-off as a result. Such individuals are skilled communicators, enjoy helping others succeed, are comfortable with diversity and manage conflict constructively. They are good empathetic listeners. They introduce new perspectives and strive for continuous improvement. They also seek active feedback and are reflective, and therefore have greater awareness of their strengths and weaknesses. The advantage of such employees to enterprises is that they perform well in first-time or novel situations, can build, lead and manage high performance teams, all very critical in a VUCA environment. But the problem is 'how does one develop such a superman?' Is there a fixed recipe that suits all purposes?

To develop agile and resilient employees, the only competency that will matter is continuous learning. As Jack Welch, the legendary former CEO of General Electric (GE), said, 'An organization's ability to learn, and translate that learning into action rapidly, is the ultimate competitive advantage.' Dr John Sullivan stresses that

> [T]here should be a clarity to everyone that in a world of constant obsolescence, knowledge, skills, tools, and practices have an extremely limited shelf life. Instead of relying on experience, training or education, the employees will be required to 'unlearn' yesterday's obsolete practices on a continuous basis and to seek new knowledge using the social trends and technology of the day. [3]

Unlearning and reverse learning are both imperative for existence in a globally competitive world driven by VUCA where acquiring dynamic capabilities is a must. In this business environment, the only key competence, which can effectively counter continuous obsolescence, is for a continuous learner to synthesize, apply and create new knowledge. The continuous learning competency is the bedrock for building a 'learning organization', a concept various firms such as Google, Toyota, Pixar Studios, Netflix, Nike and Apple have embedded since their inception.

Here, there is a point to build forward and that is an openness to learning is imperative.

Accepting obsolescence of knowledge and experience is quite hard. If one wants to be successful in a world of chaos, innovation and constant obsolescence, it needs to realise that 'yesterday's answers' are not only rapidly losing their value, but reliance upon them may be a liability. To be successful enjoying job security, each one will have to become a 'learning machine'. Hence, if you want to make your organization a successful one in a chaotic world, just come forward and declare 'continuous learning' to be the organization's No. 1 core competency and priority. [3]

What was best for yesterday is obsolete in a VUCA world. The mind needs to be fine-tuned, receptive to new thoughts, anticipate change and then synthesize with new knowledge as a continuous learner.

If you have decided that continuous learning or life-long learning is for you, then what is the way forward? Should you join in-house or external training programme every now and then and hope the road will lead you to upgrade or renew your skills and competencies to tackle new challenges? Unfortunately, that is not enough! There is always a time lag between the contents of the training programme and the real needs. They get obsolete as soon as you leave the course. If the training cannot be put in the work immediately, the contents get shifted to the backside of the memory, like a book which we no longer need gets shifted to the far corners of our bookcase. Over time, we forget it.

At a pharmaceutical company, medical representatives and managers were often called to the corporate training centre to learn new products, which are on the launch pad. The training usually started about three months prior to launch. When the tests were conducted, the trainees retained 90 per cent information on day 1, 50 per cent in week 1, 30 per cent on month 1 and only 10 per cent on month 3 when product launch took place. Again, the best training programmes can only address a fraction of the work performance issues in an organization. Training can only help to develop skills and knowledge if we know in advance what these are. In many cases, more so in a VUCA world, we don't know what our future performance needs will be. In such cases, where should an employee go to get to know his/her work performance skills and competencies? The company leadership generally has few answers. The very reason that training and development budgets are among the first to be axed when a company is passing through lean patch itself shows the importance of these activities.

In a VUCA world, knowledge is becoming more abstract, conceptual, distributed and complex. We need social and thinking skills for complex contexts and we should know how to hone these skills through practice.

The famed educational psychologist and Harvard Professor Howard Gardner in his book *Five Minds for the Future* [4] argues the need for developing the following five minds, encapsulating skills, values, attitudes and knowledge if we are to succeed in a VUCA world. These are:

1. The Disciplined Mind
   We should be educated or trained in at least one subject such as history, mathematics etc. or a profession such as law or management in such a way where we acquire

mastery in that discipline. Learning here does not only mean memorizing the facts and figures but also inculcating the habit and attitude for learning any discipline such as curiosity, questioning, inquiry, exploration, investigation, experimentation, analysis and the generation and testing of hypotheses. Mastery of discipline also means the need to revisit occasionally to improve performance. This mastery should be seen as gateways, which will be used across domains. If history is your domain, the aim is to learn the skills and thinking of a historian, not only memorizing factual knowledge. If not, your knowledge of, for example, Mughal history cannot be applied to analyse another situation such as the Civil War in Iraq.

2. The Synthesizing Mind

   A synthesizing mind has the ability to make a sense of disparate information by seeking connections. Here the mind takes information from various sources, understands and evaluates the acquired information objectively and puts it together in ways that make sense to the synthesizer and to others. It is the ability to join the dots, to see patterns, to sieve the relevant and ignore the irrelevant and to see contrasts. For example, conceiving and executing projects is in the realm of a synthesizing mind. Therefore, if people from different subject domains and past experience work together on a project, it enhances the project immensely.

   Bill Clinton has also acknowledged that intellect is good unless it completely paralyzes one's ability to undertake critical decisions because the decision-maker might visualize too many complexities. Thus, according to him, presidents need to have a synthesizing intelligence kind of ability.

The connect between disciplines and professions is increasing, and the artificial boundaries are gradually cracking. Thus, the ability to synthesize ideas is an extremely vital skill required for future, a skill basically leading to innovative leadership. Such a mind requires an understanding of interdisciplinary subjects beyond the individual ones. Such a mind is required to leverage the value of teams made up of different specialists.

3. The Creative Mind

A creative mind is capable of breaking new ground, developing new ideas and asking new questions. It brings in newer ideas, poses unfamiliar questions, pushes fresh ways of thinking and arrives at unexpected answers. We can see around that creative dimension of work is emerging to dominate the workplace as we gradually shift more to the knowledge economy. If you are only mastering disciplines 1 and 2, you can soon be replaced by a software or robot.

For example, India's third largest information technology (IT) services firm Wipro expects its headcount to come down by about 47,000 or 30 per cent in the next three years as it moves on to automation, artificial intelligence (AI) and digital services, primarily automation of BPO services which is one of the biggest employers of IT Services in India. Other firms such as Cognizant, etc. are following the same track. It is a warning sign for employees in an industry that used to hire, until very recently, thousands of employees every year.

4. The Respectful Mind

A respectful mind recognizes the differences between individuals, groups and cultures; a person with such mindset learns to appreciate diversity. Differences need to be respected and the earlier this is achieved, the better. It requires responding sympathetically and constructively to differences among groups; seeking to understand and work with those who are different; extending beyond mere tolerance and political correctness. The respectful mind leverages talents beyond gender, class, colour and religious differences among people.

5. The Ethical Mind

And finally, an ethical mind considers how one can serve several purposes beyond self-interest. This mindset actively considers the 'common good' for the wider community, particularly when put under challenging situations or complex dilemmas. Many companies are encouraging employees to seek fulfilment in corporate social responsibility (CSR) activities. Many companies such as Zara are taking issues like sustainability beyond the law of the land. Leaders such as Dick Fuld, former CEO of Lehman Brothers, and Kenneth Lay, former Chairman of Enron, people without ethical anchors, not only go down themselves but also take their organizations down.

The last two are key characteristics of future leaders.

A timely advice from Professor Gardner is that individuals with no mastery of these said disciplines shall not be able to succeed at any kind of demanding workplace. Hence, they will be cornered and restricted to menial tasks only.

Bill Gates, Andy Grove and Steve Jobs brought to their individual jobs some kind of added disciplines, which Professor Gardner had just referred to. None of the three mentioned industry leaders were the type of well-rounded business managers. Usually, the top international business schools attempt to produce high-end thinkers. However, Gates, Grove and Jobs had no formal business training and this was often reflected. All three have widely exhibited behaviour which experts on leadership would term as 'incomplete' and at times counterproductive.

Although willing to be proved wrong, each of the CEOs typically has intended to be seen himself as the smartest person in the vicinity. They could all be harsh, even unfair, towards their subordinates, but they built cultures that encouraged independent thoughts followed by fierce debates and sometimes personal confrontation.

However, all three exhibited unique strengths that profoundly affected their companies. Gates brought to Microsoft a deeper understanding of software as a technology and as a business; Grove brought to Intel an intense commitment to instil an 'engineering-like' discipline in management and operations; and Jobs brought to Apple a unique sense of product design, with an intuitive understanding of how to make complex technology accessible to the non-technical person. All three of them brought three different types of skills, which became the foundation and core strength of their respective organizations.

These strengths provided each CEO with a 'personal anchor' that grounded their contributions to the company and thus helped shape the way their organizations have evolved. The anchors drove their day-to-day focus as CEOs and guided their strategic thinking as well as decisions. The core values and differential priorities they embodied became elevated into organizational routines and competencies that remain in place even today at Microsoft, Intel and Apple [5].

People generally confuse talent with skill. Talent is an inherent aptitude for a particular discipline. Skill, on the other hand, is what happens when you cultivate talent. It is mastery over a discipline: expertise and achievement as a result of good, old-fashioned time, energy and hard work. Many talented singers give up as they do not possess the discipline to devote several hours a day in practice or *riyaz*, something which a top singer like Lata Mangeshkar did throughout her active singing life. Many talented people do not rise to the top of their potential because they are unable or unwilling to put in the required effort to convert talent into skill, that is, mastery of the five disciplines. Your talent might get you an entry, but skill is what will take you going forward in the peaks and troughs of life's journey.

It is often quoted that Bill Gates and Paul Allen did not finish college. However, what is not generally known is the depth of skill they acquired at school is beyond what the college could provide. Lakeside School, a private school both went to, had a computer at a time when it was not available even in major universities. Both spent hundreds of hours mastering their computer skills which they utilized in creating disk operating system (MS-DOS) for PCs, the beginning of their business success. This was 'the disciplined mind' at work.

Charles Darwin, an eminent biologist, during a visit to Galapagos group of islands in South America made a keen observation. He saw that the species of a finch bird on one island was different from that from another island. On further examination, he deciphered that within a few generations, the beaks of these birds had altered rapidly in both size and shape, accommodating evolutionary changes in their food sources and the environment they were living in. Thus, Darwin theorized that the different species likely came from one common ancestor yet all had adapted over time to their unique environment, especially the type of food available. In the process, these birds had transformed to a completely different set of birds. This keen observation planted the seed for his theory of evolution with its core message: survival of the fittest.

Darwin clearly understood that 'the fittest' was not necessarily the most aggressive or dominant of any kind of species but those who were able to adapt to changes in their environment.

To gain this insight, Darwin too cultivated the disciplined and synthesizing mind. Since childhood, he pursued botany and zoology, despite his father sending him first to a medical school for a career in medicine and next to a college of theology for a career as a clergyman. Fortunately, he failed at both places and continued to return to his passion for biology.

This rapid adaptation, being the key to survival, is true also for humans. We are also looking at the slow demise of regular nine-to-five job with lifelong job security as well as the disappearance of some sectors of the economy altogether and are faced with the same choice: evolve or face career extinction. Psychologist Nacie Carson in her book *The Finch Effect* says

> As humans, one of our main evolutionary advantages is that we can adapt to changes in our lifetime, learning from and teaching each other to accelerate our adaptation. And we use this strength to keep honing our strategies as our environment changes. So, a brilliant feature of the Finch Effect is that its strategies are teachable and replicable: once you know them, you can use them to adapt to any change in the job market, from current circumstances to those that will arise in the future. [6]

However, in one way, we humans differ from finches. We find the process of change and adaptation thereof uncomfortable and fear it. We shut our eyes to the inevitable and hope it does not happen or it is temporary in nature. Nacie Carson calls this mindset vocational Darwinism. No job or career is safe and the only way is take hold of life and adapt. However, we as humans have one advantage compared to finch as adaptation is the kind of change that you make happen, for adaptation implies a conscious response to shifts in your environment. There is something comforting in that fact: adaptation is the change that we control. Adaptability—being agile, flexible and open—is the most important career skill that any of us can master in our modern world. In this case, we control the change; it is a change that we desire. Career success is in your hands and no job market, be it a good one or a bad one, is going to define who you are as a professional or keep you from moving forward. Adaptability is resilience. It is ownership. It is proactivity. It is being the master of your fate and captain of your professional soul [6].

We are now living in the age of vocational Darwinism, the impact of radical change on our jobs and people must evolve to adapt to changing times by taking responsibility for their own professional development and staying relevant. The most important skill today is the ability to quickly acquire new skills. This is true to the greenhorns as well as the CEOs. In fact, the higher you go, the more isolated you become, surrounded by people who are unwilling to share the bad news, or be critical of your shortcomings. The leader must proactively sound out people to encourage debate and seek advice.

Learning is an extremely critical part of working within a knowledge economy. Learning continuously and sharing this acquired knowledge will be more important than showing up on time at the office. Continuous learning will also disrupt all existing hierarchies, as power will shift to those with greater knowledge or skills. Leadership through influence and respect will replace command and control to retain creative worker. There will be a complete disruption at the organizational level but one can create new work and learning models to help in dealing with this next phase of evolution at the workplace. Individuals have to take control of their learning in a world where they are connected, mobile and global, on a 24×7 basis.

The market for knowledge worker will continue to be impacted by digitalization, and there is both anxiety as well as optimism. Digitalization will bring flexibility and freedom to the knowledge worker in comparison to the antiquated work model of the industrial age.

For example, garment is one of the top exports from India but has remained stagnant for some years. The production of garments which is labour-intensive is moving to countries with lower labour cost such as Bangladesh and Vietnam. A skirt or a pair of pant retailing for $100 in the high street shops may bring only $10–15 to the manufacturer as they do not own their brands. Even jobs in these low-cost countries are at risk as robotic manufacturing debuts. The first fully robotic plant is coming up in the United States to manufacture T-shirts, and Adidas has also built a fully automatic plant to make shoes. Even Exide Industries in India has started a project to produce batteries fully manufactured by robots to eliminate any inconsistency in quality due to human operations. However, the need for knowledge workers who add value through designing, marketing and branding will always remain.

To gain leadership in these areas, we need a different type of worker who uses knowledge to create value rather than only labour. The country's future lies in focus on creating high-value jobs in pre-manufacturing services such as research, engineering and design by capitalizing on our comparative advantage—actual or potential—given the availability of low-cost technically qualified manpower. The Internet of Things (IoT) is another big opportunity to tap.

This change requires a radical overhaul of our education system where critical thinking and analysis take the place of rote learning and passing in examinations. Even with the best of education, much of the learning takes place in the early years of corporate life through on-the-job training and learning, and hopefully should continue throughout a person's life. One way that this valuable knowledge is acquired in the workplace is via informal learning experiences or mechanisms. This type of learning can be termed as an embedded one. This can be acquired or learned through a self-directed learning experience or percolated down from our colleagues.

Studies show that informal learning accounts for between 70 and 95 per cent of workplace learning. This continuous learning may be accomplished through mentoring, consulting or coaching. Technology can also be deployed that can facilitate this informal knowledge transfer by including virtual learning support groups, instant messaging, expert networks, mentor and coaching networks. There is a need for transiting to looser hierarchies and stronger networks if organization's knowledge has to remain relevant and useful to the organization. The pace of change and the level of complexity are outpacing the ability to push the training needed for an agile workforce. Connections would become more important than content in the organization of the future.

Learning takes place everywhere in the workplace. Beyond training, professionals have a need to connect and collaborate on a real-time basis, especially to make sense of the information overload. That time is gone when the employer took care of all your learning and skills enhancement needs. They will continue to do undertake some interventions, as is currently being done through re-skilling in the IT industry but looking at the rate of change taking place in the business environment, we must be self-reliant to integrate our learning in and out of the workplace.

Professor Sarah-Jayne Blakemore, a leading social neuroscientist, states

> that the idea on the brain being fixed in early childhood, which was a strong belief up until fairly recently, is completely wrong. There's no potential evidence of the brain being set and that it can't change after early childhood. On the contrary, the brain undergoes a systematic development passing through adolescence, into the 20s and 30s, and carries on, no matter how old one becomes. [7]

Cognitive skills are the core skills our brain uses to think, read, learn, remember, reason and pay attention. These continue to develop through our lives as learning never ends.

To improve our own and our organization's learning quotient, we need to look at ways to be more self-directed, social and agile learners, and it is time to take responsibility for our own learning.

One can learn from anyone, from any event and at any time and place. These opportunities are all around us to continuously propel us to excel ourselves in our performance, provided we develop a healthy attitude for learning and come with a positive mindset. This book is a mosaic of learning tools and guides. Thus, none of us should ever quit learning. There should be a thirst for acquiring knowledge and that we should do our best to quench it through continuous learning. One must try learning something new every day. Sometimes the learning can be trivial, sometimes it is profound. Regardless, one should keep on learning. What is the source of continuous learning? Let us start the journey, investigate and examine what continuous learning implies and how it can position a learner in a VUCA world.

References

1. Johannsen, Bob. 2007. *Getting There Early: Sensing the Future to Compete in the Present*. San Francisco: Berrett-Koehier Publishers.
2. Marcus, Lucy. 2015, 15 January. *How to Prepare for the Unknown Unknowns*. Available at https://www.weforum.org/agenda/2015/01/how-to-prepare-for-the-unknown-unknowns/ (accessed 5 February 2018).
3. Sullivan, Dr John. 2010, 6 September. *Think Piece: The Only Competency That Will Matter Is Continuous Learning*. Available at https://drjohnsullivan.com/articles/continuous-learning-competency/ (accessed 5 February 2018).
4. Gardner, Howard. 2006. *Five Minds for the Future*. Harvard Business Press.

5. Yoffie, David B. and Michael A. Cusumano. 2015, May. How Bill Gates, Andy Grove and Steve Jobs Found Success Without Business Training. *Fast Company*. Available at https://www.fastcompany.com/3044952/how-bill-gates-andy-grove-and-steve-jobs-found-success-without-busine (accessed 5 February 2018).

6. Carson, Nacie. 2012. *The Finch Effect*. Hoboken, NJ: Wiley.

7. Brockman, John (ed.). 2013. *Thinking*. New York, NY: Harper Perennial.

Chapter 2
An Unexpected Learner *

*Without the vision of a goal, a man cannot manage his own life,
much less the lives of others...*

—Genghis Khan

Journey of an Unexpected Learner

---

* This chapter is largely based on Jack Weatherford's *Genghis Khan
and the Making of the Modern World*, published by Three Rivers
Press in 2004 at Carmarthen, UK.

Learning agility is the ability and willingness to learn from every opportunity and subsequently apply that learning to perform successfully under different conditions, and no one epitomes this characteristic more than Mongol conqueror Genghis Khan. He would have been a very successful multinational CEO in a VUCA world. He embodied agility, adaptability and resilience to the full. In fact, Genghis Khan exhibits characteristics mentioned in Professor Gardner's *Five Minds for the Future* to a large extent.

Genghis Khan, the 12th-century Mongol conqueror, is a prime example of an agile and resilient lifelong learner. He is depicted as a barbarian tyrant by European historians. We can learn more about leadership from Genghis Khan than any other figure of historic interest, as most that we know about him is distorted. For early beginners, it has been evidenced that he abolished torture, embraced religious freedom continuously, attempted to unite disparate tribes, disliked aristocratic privileges, operated his kingdom meritocratically and appreciated learning. It is surprising to learn that even today, when many parts of the world treat women as second-class citizens and deny basic rights, Genghis was a supporter of women's rights and their equal stature in Mongol society. He said, 'Let us reward our female offspring' [1].

He was also one of the greatest conqueror and a general, ruling a self-made kingdom of nearly 12 million square miles that lasted in several parts for nearly seven centuries. Certainly, he was a violent and warlike king, but not for himself. The Mongols found no honour in fighting but only on winning. Victory was considered their main purpose and hence they did whatever came by to get it. However, they focused equally on building peace with the same intensity. Thus, while other conquerors around the world died facing violence, Khan died as an old man surrounded by his affable family [2].

He was a man of contrasts on one hand, conniving, ambitious and ruthless, and on the other, humble, generous and loyal. However, in comparison, he showed less barbarity than the Civil War in Rwanda or the holocaust of the Second World War and the daily horrors of ISIS. He was much more than a tyrant. The late Professor Owen Lattimore claimed that Genghis Khan was one of the greatest strategists witnessed and produced by this world. He further said, 'as a military genius, he was able to take over new techniques and improvise upon. Genghis stood above Alexander the Great, Hannibal, Caesar, Attila and Napoleon' [3]. *The Washington Post*, in 1995, termed Genghis Khan as its 'Man of the Millennium'. He was described as 'an apostle of extremes, who embodied the half-civilised, half-savage duality of the human race'. Tongue-in-cheek, *The Washington Post* rejected Columbus for the millennial honour as 'somewhat boring' [4].

With Mongols accomplishing so much, it hardly seemed surprising and that the first author in the English language, Geoffrey Chaucer, devoted one of the longest stories in *The Canterbury Tales* to the Asian conqueror, Mongolian, Genghis Khan. He candidly described the undisguised accomplishments of the Mongolian conqueror [5].

Fate was not kind to Genghis. When he was only nine years old, his father, a tribal chief, was assassinated. Genghis was too young to succeed and the successor saw in him a rival, a future claimant, and expelled him along with his mother and two brothers from the clan, hoping that without tribal support, they will die in the wilderness.

The harsh environment taught him early lessons in survival along with the full range of human emotions, ambition, cruelty, desire, etc. He even killed his elder half-brother; eventually captured and then enslaved by a rival clan, yet he managed to escape. Fate never handed Genghis Khan to his destiny rather he designed it for himself.

An interesting secret history of the Mongols recollects on how Temujin escaped wearing a wooden cangue, a collar-like implement, which entrapped his head and two arms plunged into a river. By intelligently using the cangue as a pillow, he lay on the bed of the river and kept his head above water. His narrow escape had been cleverly and intelligently planned and calmly executed. The night of a feast was purposely chosen, while there were careless guards around. Rather than taking this opportunity to flee, he acted calmly, bought time and hid. Under such horrifying extraordinary conditions as told and assumed, the young boy reflected an instinct for survival and resilience. This careful planning, self-control, understanding of people, the awareness of his innate powers over others, reduced and controlled impulsiveness were all the greater qualities that he was henceforth to develop over the next decades.

Riding around 50 miles every day on a horse, he acquired a tacit learning that the 15 feet of silk cloth tied tightly around the midriff kept the internal organs in place thus preventing any kind of nausea. Having dried yoghurt in his pocket and keeping it handy for long treks, when there was no time to stop over and cook a meal, was yet another learning he mastered in his journey. Besides this, the practicality of having a thick Mongol robe, called a *deel*, when riding on wooden saddles made the ruthless journey somewhat comfortable. He had countless episodes of being lost in the tiring journey and in an adventurous geography yet each passage gave him new lessons on directions, navigation, tenacity and the patience of waiting. Over a period, Genghis Khan intuitively learned on how intimately the Mongols knew their own world and he could, without fail, trust their astute judgement, physical stamina and generosity. As he learned, so did his confidence grew as a leader and these lessons were invaluable when he decided to expand his empire.

Many individuals and small groups were drawn to Temujin, often defying the leaders of their clans who had not yet bowed to him. With increasing reputation and an image of a generous leader, who inspired and rewarded loyalty, Khan's standing grew tremendously.

Genghis Khan, an illiterate (writing had not yet reached Mongols), was a product of his times where life as a shepherd was a daily struggle for survival and where the chiefs shared the rigorous life of miseries, hunger and privations of their people.

Genghis soon understood that warfare was not at all a sporting contest matching between rivals. In fact, it was a complete pitch of one person against another. It was understood that the victory did not come to the one who played by the rules but to the one who made the rules and imposed them on his enemy. Triumph was never partial. It had to be complete, total, exclusive and undeniable or it was nothing. His strategy was to frighten his opponents into surrendering without a battle, benefiting his own troops, whose lives he valued. Those frightened into surrender were spared violence [6].

He used terror and surprise as major tactics of battles. He pursued peace with equal vigour through adherence to certain principles to create loyalty among his people. His experience of exploiting people and technology was gained as a result of more than 40 years of warfare. His genius at the battlefield, ability to inspire loyalty and ability to organize a worldwide empire were not acquired at any particular stage in life but through lifelong incremental and continuous learning. Genghis Khan was not born with divine powers or formal education. His success was the result of a disciplined approach to practical and logical learning, experimentation and adaptation, sometimes from failures.

Mongols were divided into numerous tribes with a common culture but continuously fighting and raiding among themselves. Additionally, until Genghis Khan gained control over the Uyghur people, the Mongolians did not have a writing system. Genghis, however, could visualize the importance of the written word and apprenticed his youngest son to learn writing from Uyghurs. As he gained new territory and came in touch with established states, Genghis Khan started making changes in governance. He learnt governance from captured Turks, Chinese and others, and began to devise a more stable system that could contribute to a more orderly government. Two examples illustrate the learner side of his personality.

The average Mongol tribe numbered 100 to 300 warriors. When Genghis started unifying the tribes, his army gradually increased to thousands and ultimately about 200,000 and his empire four times larger than that of Alexander the Great. He had little idea of managing a large army and there was nobody to mentor him. He had to learn basic field tactics such as encircling, feigning retreat, signalling system, etc., through experimentation, and trial and error. He was harsh on people who would not submit to the discipline of transforming from a horde to an army. He created a disciplined cavalry moving in coordinated units, which laid the foundation of his global empire.

Genghis Khan, with only the insights of his experiences, transformed his hordes into a modern disciplined and trained army. He divided his army into decimal units:

1. The *arban* (a unit comprising of 10 warriors) is its own council

2. Ten *noyat* (officers) of the *arban* form the council of the *jegun* (unit of 100 warriors)

3. Ten *noyat* of the *jegun* forming the council of the *mingon* (unit of 1,000 warriors)

4. Ten *noyat* of the *mingon* forming the council of the *tumen* (unit of 10,000 warriors)

5. The *noyan* (generals, princes, commanders of 10,000 warriors) forming the council of the Khan

A hierarchical organization, the army moved in long columns sometimes separated by great distances and kept in touch by swift riders. The army consisted only of cavalry. There was no infantry.

All acts of bravery and elevated skills were rewarded graciously. In one battle, an enemy warrior killed the horse on which Genghis Khan was riding. When this warrior was apprehended, he admitted killing the horse, yet Genghis pardoned and took him into the service with the nickname Jebe or 'arrow'. Jebe rose to become one of Temujin's greatest generals of all times [7].

Khan also deployed subterfuge as a strategy by lighting countless campfires, mounting dummies on their spare horses as a mechanism of deceit. He even used trailing branches and bushes to stir up dust. With this, the Mongols created an impression that their numbers were far more than they actually were. This indeed was an intellectual mechanism of deceiving the enemy and building surprise at all times. He was a VUCA learner and demonstrated the power of knowledge creation and continuous learning ability under turbulent times. In a number of cases, they won against significantly larger enemies.

His genius also lay in the way he empowered his officers, something we are only implementing today in evolved organizations, making way for agility in campaigns, a hallmark of the Mongols. He allowed his officers great discretion in carrying out the battle orders, improvising as they fought, as long as the overall strategic objectives were met. Genghis' armies were thus freed from overly rigid discipline and micromanagement, which have hampered the operations of armies in entire history.

Genghis Khan used to organize long public discussion before embarking on a major campaign. There was representation from and within the community in each process. Most importantly, everyone who became a part of the Khan's journey clearly understood what and why they were fighting for. As a principle, the soldiers were expected to obey on the battlefield. Even the lowest ranks were generously treated as junior partners and were expected to understand the combined endeavour with a voice in it. The senior members met frequently in large public meetings whereby issues were discussed openly. They subsequently went to their respective units to continue the discussions with the other lower ranking warriors. Thus, to have a full commitment from each warrior, it became pertinent that each of them, from the highest to the lowest, participate and know where each one stood in the larger plan of events [6].

Genghis Khan inordinately absorbed the free-flowing knowledge of his expanded geography and thus supported his fighting men for every terrain of learning. He intelligently formed specialized support units for his army, which comprised with a balance of Persian and Chinese physicians to attend the wounded, Chinese engineers to run catapults and siege engines, supply officers and the signal corps. There was a diversity as well as optimum competence required to lead a winning army. Interestingly, he established a sophisticated yet practical signalling system that included drums, flags and smoke by day and torches by night. He was much ahead of his time.

Part of Genghis Khan's great success was due to his great devotion to pragmatic principles. If it worked, Genghis Khan had no reluctance to part with tradition and adopt a better strategy, whether it was his own creation or an established practice of another nation.

Many of his best generals and field commanders who were included in his winning team belonged to conquered nations. As Genghis conquered more territory, he came in contact with the bureaucracy and intelligentsia of the conquered nations, especially Chinese who had developed the systems required to run a large empire. He unabashedly used any new method or scheme which he found useful to run his growing empire, often overruling his own people. He respected merit and promoted flexible problem-solvers with a demonstrated ability to learn.

On training and ever-readiness, Genghis Khan made it clear that every Mongol shall learn riding a horse from the very age of three. Second, by the age of five, he should stand in the stirrups at full gallop and be able to effectively hit a target from 100 yards. He knew that capability had to be infused both in mindset and in physical self. When Mongols were unoccupied with war, they were told to devote themselves to hunting. There was no room for complacency where learning stopped. The objective was not so on the chase or hunt but train the warriors in acquiring strength and gain familiarity with the drawing of the bow and other exercises.

He learnt how to conduct the siege of fortified cities. Genghis and his army lived and fought on open grasslands and he had no experience of laying siege to and conquering forts. Until he reached the walls of the Chinese cities, he had never seen a stone building. Unlike Chinese generals, who with time had grown up within their respective cities with access to centuries-old besieging techniques, Genghis Khan, on the contrary, had to invent and reinvent his own methods for survival. He developed many tactics including cutting supply lines, diverting rivers and operating his newly acquired Chinese siege engines. Not all experiments succeeded but lessons were learnt. When he attacked the fortified city of Tangut capital, he used one unorthodox method of diverting a channel of the Yellow River to flood it. This was a unique experience. With no experience in engineering, the Mongols, however, succeeded in diverting the river but eventually wiped out their own camp instead of the Tangut. The fast learning from this early failure was that in future, the Mongols would repeat this method, but each time they would be more adept at it and use it more judiciously and successfully. Ultimately, they perfected siege warfare to such a high degree and precision that Genghis ended the era of walled cities.

It was not only the walled cities, but the innovative fighting techniques introduced by Genghis Khan obsoleted the heavily armoured knights of medieval Europe, thereby replacing them with a disciplined light cavalry moving speedily in coordinated units.

In every battle, he learned something new, bringing new ideas into an evolving doctrine of tactics, strategies and weapons. He always introduced something new in each battle.

Instead of fielding large armies of foot soldiers, the Mongol armies comprised of mobile cavalry that could be swiftly activated. Genghis Khan leveraged this mobility to the hilt, both tactically and strategically. His enemies could not match his speed and precision. He could move through a territory sometimes 100 miles in a day and on the battle-field. At times, these Mongols were infamous for staging false retreats and drawing larger forces into an ambush. They emerged as stealth fighters, deploying an effective flanking strategy.

An army composed of horses is nothing new for Mongol tribes but Genghis Khan adapted the tactics of conquered people and improvised his own. In China, he incorporated siege of fortified cities which allowed him to attack larger cities. When he entered Middle East Islamic countries, he allowed religious practices to continue which attracted various factions to join his armies against oppressive and dogmatic rulers.

His pursuit of lifelong learning comes out clearly through his efforts to teach his sons. What is surprising is that unlike most conquerors who had come before him and followed him, he displayed a keen sense of self-awareness. Genghis taught his warriors that the first key to leadership was to have self-control, particularly the mastery of pride, which was something more difficult than to subdue a wild lion and anger, which was more difficult to defeat than the greatest wrestler. He warned them that 'if one can't swallow your pride, you can't lead'. He emphasized and admonished them not to think of themselves as the strongest or smartest. Even the highest mountain had animals that step on it, he warned. When the animals climb to the top of the mountain, they are even higher than it is [6].

Genghis advised his sons about talking too much. His emphasis was on a leader who should demonstrate his thoughts and opinions through his actions and not through his words. He stressed upon his sons the importance of having a vision supplemented by goals and plans without which you cannot fulfil your destiny. Also, keep the welfare of your people above yours.

Genghis lived a simple life and warned his sons about the folly of pursuing a life of luxury with fine clothes, fast horses and beautiful women. This is a sure way of straying from your vision, losing everything you have achieved.

In one of the most important lessons he learnt, he shared with his sons that conquering an army is not similar to conquering a nation. An army can be conquered with superior tactics and men, but a nation can be conquered effectively only by winning the hearts of the people. This may sound idealistic, yet he followed with even more practical advice that even though the Mongol Empire should be one, the subject people should never be allowed to unite as one: 'People conquered on different sides of the lake should be ruled on different sides of the lake.' Such learnings showed his appreciation of diversity [6].

Genghis Khan matured as a leader as he went along. The Khan frequently consulted outside experts for his own personal development as a leader, especially later in his life. He accepted that outside knowledge emanating beyond his boundaries must also be understood and adopted, if necessary. It may follow adaptation with time and purpose. Even at the pinnacle of his success, he sought advice from trusted advisors on diverse areas—be it spirituality or how to prevent his people from growing 'soft' as his empire grew. He blamed the decadent life of rulers for their defeat at his hands. Despite the huge wealth he accumulated, Genghis lived a simple life and ate the same food as common soldiers and horse herders. He exercised moderation in all his actions. He had a great regard for talented men, whether Mongols or from other lands, and pursued a relationship with his officers based on mutual respect.

He invited a Chinese monk Ch'ang Ch'un to visit him and in his invitation letter, which gives a rare insight into his humble personality, wrote:

Heaven has abandoned China owing to its haughtiness and extravagant luxury. But I, living in the northern wilderness, have not inordinate passions. I hate luxury and exercise moderation. I have only one coat and one food. I eat the same food and am dressed in the same tatters as my humble herdsmen. I consider the people my children and take an interest in talented men as if they were my brothers. We always agree in our principles, and we are always united by mutual affection. At military exercises, I am always in the front, and in time of battle am never behind. In the space of seven years, I have succeeded in accomplishing great work and uniting the whole world in one empire. I have not myself distinguished qualities....

Commiserate the people in the present situation of
affairs, or have pity upon me, and communicate to me the
means of preserving life. I shall serve thee myself. I hope
that at least thou wilt leave me a trifle of thy wisdom.
Say only one word to me and I shall be happy. In this
letter, I have briefly expressed my thoughts, and hope that
thou wilt understand them. I hope also that thou, having
penetrated the principles of the great tao, sympathisest
with all that is right, and wilt not resist the wishes of the
people. [8]

Ultimately, Genghis Khan showed that leadership is not
something you are born with or is an innate quality but
one which can be learnt and perfected through diligent
development, study and application.

If we have to choose one business leader of the
20th century who was an equal of Genghis Khan in life
and achievement, it would be Steve Jobs. He was one such
self-taught leader who continued to learn throughout his
life. More than Apple, the founding and steering of Pixar
Animation Studios shows the extent of similarity with
Genghis Khan.

His life's learning comes out clearly at the commence-
ment address he delivered at Stanford University on 12 June
2005 [9].

He dropped out of college after six months. He was not
ready to spend his parents' hard-earned savings on tuitions
when '[I] had no idea what I wanted to do with my life and
no idea how college was going to help me figure it out'.
However, he continued to drop into classes which interested him, following his curiosity and intuition, one of

which was on calligraphy. He used the learning to design the interface of his first Macintosh computer.

His life was tough, same as Genghis Khan's early experiences. He ate well once a week at Hare Krishna Temple to which he walked seven miles each way.

At the age of 30, he was fired from Apple, the company which he helped found. He recalls that

> [G]etting fired from Apple was the best thing that could have ever happened to me. The heaviness of being successful was replaced by the lightness of being a beginner again, less sure about everything. It freed me to enter one of the most creative periods of my life.

This led to his founding of two firms NeXt and Pixar Animation Studios.

Pixar Studios has the structure and culture to ride out successfully in a VUCA world. There are no stars in Pixar. In other studios, director is the star and everybody bows to him. In Pixar, movie is the star and even the junior most employee who has just joined can watch the sequences and offer critique. It is a merit-based organization where your power does not come from your title or position, but your ideas and innovation.

The result is visible in Pixar's. Consider: the company made 15 feature films till 2015 but of those, seven have won the Academy Award for Best Animated Feature Film. In total, it has 12 Oscars and another 30 nominations. Its output has grossed more than $9 billion worldwide.

The leadership principle is to surround yourself with smart people, then allow them to speak freely. Candour is encouraged. Deference = self-censorship.

Even Pixar film goes through an intensive process of iteration, testing and further iteration. When it isn't working, share it; you never know where a breakthrough is going to come from [10].

Therefore, what is expected out of a learner? The life of Genghis Khan exhibits the process of learning and embedding it in one's behaviour, and also encouraging it in others, which are core to developing competencies in the learner. Perhaps, no one is born perfect, as an encyclopaedia for all weather terrain. Each learning experience, which is tacit, must be therefore passed over to generations candidly as handholding and lifelong learning. Therefore, it comes to an interesting dialogue as how to educate and when to educate on the learning gaps and the need to fortify knowledge.

Genghis Khan, like every individual, would have encountered different learning experiences and hence deduced the need to acquire more knowledge via constant engagement and pursuance of purpose. Transfer of knowledge is not easy, unless the one who desires to give away shares with one who needs with a similar purpose and vice versa. There must be a high level and degree of connect between the two. The learning and transfer may be formal or informal, theoretical or experiential. The skills required in both conditions are different, but what is core to the subject is that learning must be continuous and contemporary. This is a skill and an art of an agile and resilient leader.

References

1. Weatherford, Jack. 2010. *The Secret History of the Mongol Queens*. New York: Random House.
2. Holiday, Ryan. 2012, 7 May. 9 Lessons on Power and Leadership from Genghis Khan. *Forbes*. Available at https://www.forbes.com/sites/ryanholiday/2012/05/07/9-lessons-on-leadership-from-genghis-khan-yes-genghis-khan/#6c3c7f296996 (accessed 6 February 2018).
3. Onon, Urgunge. 2001. *The Secret History of the Mongols: The Life and Times of Chinggis Khan* (Translated, Annotated and with an Introduction by Urgunge Onon). London: Routledge.
4. Achenbach, Joel. 1995, 31 December. The Era of His Ways. *The Washington Post*. Available at https://www.washingtonpost.com/archive/lifestyle/1995/12/31/the-era-of-his-ways/58a4ef4c-052f-4cd3-b6ee-5e68b4159161/?utm_term=.fbcbffb49cf1 (accessed 6 February 2018).
5. Matheson, Lister M. (ed.). 2011. 'Chinggis Khan: World Conqueror'. *Icons of the Middle Ages: Medieval Masters*, 205. Santa Barbara, CA: ABC-Clio.
6. Weatherford, Jack. 2004. *Genghis Khan and the Making of the Modern World*. Carmarthen, UK: Three Rivers Press.
7. Hildinger, Erik. 1997. *Warriors of the Steppe: A Military History of Central Asia 500 BC to 1700 AD*. Cambridge, MA: Da Capo Press.
8. Bretschneider, E. 1888. *Medieval Researches from Eastern Asiatic Sources*. New York, NY: Barnes & Noble.
9. Stanford News. 2005, 12 June. '*You've Got to Find What You Love,*' Jobs Says. Available at https://news.stanford.edu/2005/06/14/jobs-061505/ (accessed 14 June 2005).
10. Franklin-Wallis, Oliver. 2015, December. Think Like Pixar: 7 Lessons From the Studio's Creative Culture. *Wired*. Available at http://www.wired.co.uk/article/pixar-lessons-film-studio-creative-business (accessed 6 February 2018).

Chapter 3
The Future of Work: The New Workplace

*It's not about the skill level or how much education you have.
Really, the primary question is, is the job on some level routine,
repetitive and predictable?*

—'The Robots Are Coming'

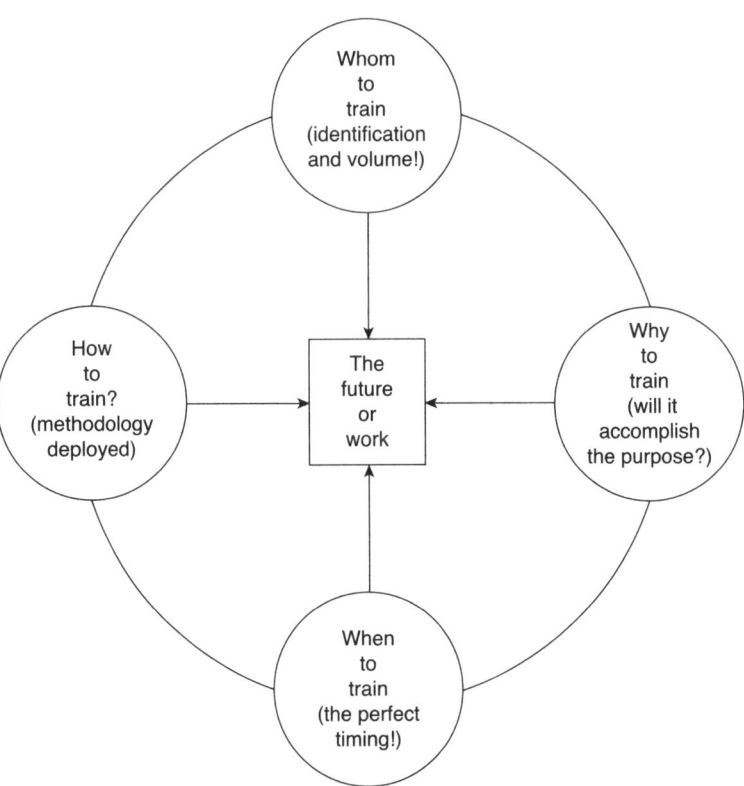

India needs to train 500 million people in the next 10 years. The half-life of a professional skill is down to five years and is shrinking fast. It makes no sense to train people on skills that will become obsolete in short order, possibly by the time the learner is out of the skills training school. The questions to ask are:

1. Whom to train? (Identification and volume!)
2. Why to train? (Reasons? Will it accomplish the purpose?)
3. When to train? (The perfect timing!)
4. How to train? (Methodology deployed)

This needs to be examined vis-à-vis to the current and forecasted scenario.

The Work Scenario Today

On Wall Street, most trading is now done by algorithms. There have been lots and lots of jobs that have disappeared already, and again the important thing is that in many cases, these are skilled jobs.

The field of law is being impacted, with algorithms that do document review taking over a lot of the more routine work that used to be done by lawyers and paralegals. Are we ready?

Wipro Ltd will use its AI platform HOLMES to automate several aspects of its so-called fixed price projects, saving up to $46.5 million and freeing around 3,000 engineers from mundane software maintenance activities (here, freeing could mean letting them go). About 30,000 of Wipro's workforce of 110,000 work in fixed price projects. For instance, Wipro is using HOLMES to help large banks approve and process loans quickly. The platform extracts a new customer's information, performs a cognitive search comparing the credit history with the bank's other customers, and authenticates and validates the loan process [1].

The news that the large number of personnel being freed up by the emergence of AI underlines the disruption that is about to hit the job market.

Most IT and ITeS companies still do not have clear ideas as to what will happen to those people being freed from current tasks. Many companies have announced lofty re-skilling targets, but according to a forecast, 600,000 (25% of total workforce) low-skilled jobs will be lost in next five years. However, at the same time, highly skilled jobs will be created for people with creative problem-solving skills and analytics, but numbers may not match.

Other industries like manufacturing are also following suit. People at all levels must start thinking about lateral shifts, multi-skilling, self-employment and other strategies to cope with the massive disruption that is on the horizon. According to a recent report by Project Management Institute, India would require seven million project managers in next 10 years. Shouldn't some of those at risk in IT and ITeS industries start working towards this end?

The future of work depends upon the changing role of human resources function from personnel management to partners in employee development, applying evolving strategies in future of work, creating environment where employees are motivated to rise to their potential, changing role of leaders focused on unlocking human potential and pushing employees to be and do their best. There is an instant need for just-in-time capabilities and learning.

Twelve Global Trends Which Will Change the Workplace

The Boston Consulting Group's (BCG) recently published research of the global work landscape has identified 12 primary forces or megatrends, which will change the workplace of tomorrow. These forces shall combiningly revolutionize the way the work is executed in firms. It will compel their leaders to rethink even if it is the most basic assumption on how their organizations should function. They will have a greater propensity to unearth newer dimensions of organizing, the way they perform and lead, along with different approaches towards recruiting, developing and positively engaging employees. With these organizations with limitless data, open boundaries, employees and machines working side by side, rapidly evolving strategies shall be a force to reckon with in attracting talent [2]. The challenges to both employees and leadership are huge.

Automation

BCG estimates that by 2050, 50 per cent of all jobs are likely to be automated in the United States (India is not far behind). Robotics and AI will replace routine work, whether factories or offices. Enterprises would need higher level of skilled talent such as programming, analytics, cloud, marketing professionals in banking, especially to open up rural areas, etc. It is already estimated that the

United States will face a shortage of over 160,000 analytics professionals by 2020. Japan is easing resident visa rules for highly skilled professionals. Many such opportunities would open up for those Indians who are continuously adapting to the dynamics of the global scenario and continuously upgrading their knowledge and skills.

Data collection and mining has been around for some time now but today, the data size has increased exponentially and would continue to do so. Companies of all sizes would have to develop or employ talent which can uncover insights from customer behaviour and experiences. They need people who can analyse and dissect using sophisticated tools and techniques. Companies would have to install systems for continuous ongoing and dynamically changing skills development.

It is certain that robotics and AI will permeate wide segments of daily life by 2025, with huge implications for a range of industries such as health care, transport and logistics, customer service and home maintenance. The cost of robots is coming down every year, allowing more companies to deploy these. Today's robots, such as Baxter by Rethink Robotics, cost only $22,000 for a basic model and are flexible and trainable. But even as the experts are largely consistent in their predictions for the evolution of technology itself, they are deeply divided on how advances in AI and robotics will impact the economic and employment picture over the next decade.

Big Data and Advanced Analytics

The shift to modern platform architectures and inexpensive computing resources makes it easier for companies to tap into new sources of data, and these data have significantly higher volumes, velocities and varieties. But modern platforms don't just produce and store new sources of data; they help create meaning.

Data is a potential source of insight and leadership, but only if companies have the right people to find meaning in it. Information is today a key resource, much more important than capital. There is no shortage of capital today but having the right people in right place certainly is. The new generation of data-driven workers must be adept in creative thinking, creating hypothesis, theorizing and exploratory data analysis, whatever their function whether marketing or supply chain to draw actionable insights.

However, employees cannot transform into data scientists without skills enhancement in data literacy as well as produce software which is user-friendly.

Access to Information and Ideas

We consider this as an ability of leaders in excavating information required whether it resides with the employees, peer groups, vendors or competitors, etc. This acquired knowledge needs to be translated into skills mandated to be an effective leader in a given VUCA situation. Being an agile learner by this interpretation implies to being able to navigate between various information sources that are literally at our fingertips, evaluate the utility and apply this information to solve problems, improving the overall performance of employees and the organization.

Simplicity in Complexity

This implies on the value and power of simplicity, the lean methodologies, its timely evolution from silos to a more holistic organization, with reduced organizational complicatedness.

Dealing with complexity is one of the key leadership challenges that any leader needs to successfully face. As humans, we tend to overcomplicate things. Since our dreams and goals tend to be so big, we believe that the road to success must be complex. We must do something so complicated and groundbreaking to be rewarded with what we want. Otherwise, wouldn't everyone be doing it? We create complex organizations with too many silos and have endless meetings and overwhelming workloads. What separates great leaders from the rest of us is that they practice the fundamentals first. It is not the complex matters—strategy, business skills or outstanding foresight. Punctuality, teamwork and work ethics are some of the simple principles they follow. Albert Einstein said that 'If you cannot explain it simply, you don't understand it enough.' Great leaders such as Jack Welch and Ted Turner take complex strategies and simplify them down into key messages and action items that everyone can follow. How good is a great mission statement if it's too complicated and difficult to follow?

The outstanding leaders are consistently focused on the things that really mattered. Like master gardeners, they recognized that careful pruning would ultimately yield stronger, more sustained results.

In 1997, Steve Jobs said, 'I'm actually as proud of the things we haven't done as the things we have done. Innovation is saying "no" to 1,000 things.' But he also succeeded in consistently simplifying the strategy into memorable themes. Apple's business strategy is 'bringing the best user experience to its customers'. That's not far from the message of its first product brochure: 'Simplicity is the ultimate sophistication'. It shows the power of simplicity, even in complex systems.

As the world becomes more complex, simplifying strategy, interdependencies, decision-making and all communication become more important than ever.

Agility and Innovation

An accelerating pace of rate of change, with increasing uncertainty and black swan events, is exponentially witnessed by organizations, thereby requiring agile development and innovation.

In today's turbulent business environment, leaders with the ability to anticipate change and make fast and effective performance decisions can enable high performing teams that drive organizational agility. Jack Welch, former CEO of GE, said, 'when the rate of change outside exceeds the rate of change inside, the end is in sight'. The leadership must constantly look at the business environment and ask: what's happening with business disruption (e.g., digital, demographic, global, security, etc.) and how can we implement leadership, team and organizational agility in our company? Here the challenge is even more complex, as companies get engaged in the vortex of innovation. If they keep pace they succeed, else they perish. Nokia is one great example of an innovative firm, succumbing to competition as it was slow to listen to customers and market-based innovations.

The New Age 'thinker' worker demands more autonomy and control over their work. Therefore, the organizations must loosen the traditional rigid line and staff structures, make it more network oriented to enable rapid consultation, team and group working, and peer learning. The organizations must create an innovative culture with space for experimentation and prototyping, testing of new ideas and a tolerance for failures. Failures should lead to learning and success. This not only requires the development of new skills and competencies but also the evolution of attitudes and behaviour on part of workers and the leadership. Such changes also help in greater employee satisfaction and foster innovation culture. The question arises, 'How do we develop such leaders?'

Agile learners exhibit a willingness and refined ability to unlearn and learn throughout their life. There is a greater tendency to continuously seek for growth opportunities and orient them towards scalable results or outcomes. They are open to change with each added new experience. With each challenge, they are eager to introduce new ideas, concepts and keep questioning the existing 'norms'. They keep flying, discovering, performing and rapidly adapting as an adventurer. These individuals also appreciate that this acquired experience does not guarantee learning; hence they occasionally pause, reflect on the past, attempting to discover why, how and what of incidents that have happened. They keep asking questions and with this continuous curiosity tend to look for answers around them, increasing their learning with agility and adaptability.

There is a tendency in judging people based on what they have done and what they know. However, yet another thought is which could be a better indicator of measuring leadership success is on how well they learn [3]. Jack Welch also says that 'An organization's ability to learn and translate that learning into action rapidly, is the ultimate competitive advantage.'

Leaders of tomorrow need to be better than the leaders they replace because the challenges are greater, the speed faster, the competition tougher and the marketplace increasingly global. In such cases, there is a greater tendency of success by organizations with learning-agile leaders as compared with others. In fact, these agile leaders rapidly adapt their leadership style as a response towards the dynamic changing business environment, whether internal or external. Thus, the agility is all about having a flexibility in changing rapidly to a given set of circumstances.

Continuously learning, agile leaders are ready to challenge the status quo. They challenge long-held assumptions with a goal to discover new and unique ways of doing things. This requires one to have new experiences, which provide perspective and an opportunity to grow one's knowledge base of understanding. Such leaders generate new ideas through their ability to view issues from multiple angles. They readily accept change and innovation.

Innovation is a culture—a culture of risk-takers, idea generators and simplifiers. People who don't give up speak up in an environment built on trust. Cultures aren't born;

they evolve, and it takes time and focus. The most innovative companies know that the best ideas start with diverse teams that bring together people from many backgrounds, with different experiences, to make things happen. This cultural integration leverages upon diverse perspectives leading to a refined level of innovations and its application. Here comes the role of the leader.

For that to happen, leaders should set the tone. They develop the vision and priorities; they convey what's important and what to focus on (simplify). They also make or break, whether or not the work environment is open and built on trust, through their transparency and authenticity. This is important if we want innovation to flourish.

New Customer Strategies

This relates to the personalization of premium products, tailored services, enhanced data security, ethics, etc.

The recent imbroglio of Airtel Payments Bank where UIDAI had to temporarily ban Bharti Airtel and Airtel Payments Bank from conducting Aadhaar-based SIM verification of mobile customers is a pointer in this direction. The action followed the practice of Bharti Airtel using the Aadhaar eKYC-based SIM verification process to open payments bank accounts of its subscribers without their consent. This embarrassment ultimately led to the ouster of Airtel Payments Bank's CEO.

The rise of mobile, social media and global information marketplace has made customers more empowered which is bringing about a change in strategy of companies to make themselves more focused on the customer. Customer insights are gleaned from such tools as data analytics and behavioural sciences. For this to happen, the leadership must unleash their workforce through imparting high-level competency, skills and thinking power. Only then can employees uncover insights to develop customer-oriented strategy.

The customer is more demanding. Do you know why? The customer is more educated due to information over-flow and it has quadrupled in the age of digitization. The expectation of satisfaction has risen; if one fails, the competition is waiting to fulfil this perceived or created gap. This is not good news for any organization, especially when most organizations are building business models with customer-centric focus.

Shifts in Resource Distribution

India is an example of a surfeit supply of poorly trained and skilled workers and a shortage of highly skilled independently thinking and innovative professionals. This is true of all major countries, whether the United States or Thailand. Skilling and re-skilling are not keeping with the fast-changing dynamic global economy. Companies are challenged to attract and retain scarce and specialized talent, which today can move wherever in the world; talent is valued. For example, in many of the free trade agreements, which India is negotiating with other countries such as ASEAN and Eurasian blocs, there is provision for free movement of people to take up assignments in each other's territories. Japan too is making provisions in its visa policies to allow highly skilled professionals get residence visa for longer term.

Rapidly growing emerging economies such as India are churning out a large number of poorly skilled young workers and professionals who are not readily employable. The challenge is to help them develop those skills, or for some young people to increase their mobility so that they can find fulfilling jobs elsewhere.

Meanwhile, millennial and Generation Z are entering the global workforce with new expectations and orientations. In their search for a healthy work-life balance and opportunities for self-expression, they are harder to please than their predecessors. They are also harder to retain.

These demographic shifts will put pressure on companies to devise entirely new ways to attract, retain and develop talent across locations and age groups. They will need to hold on to experienced older workers and find ways to facilitate the transfer of those workers' deep knowledge to incoming generations. Knowledge transfer must take place tacitly and with a great amount of speed. The newer generation must be ready to learn and acquire higher capabilities needed to scale up, both in their profession and to add value to their employers. Sharp and intelligent networking will come handy.

Skill Imbalances

This issue is connected with the new skills, the waning skill life, existing formal curricula, latecomers in the digital age and skills education, its reach, etc.

The skills and capabilities businesses require are rapidly evolving. As robotics, automation and AI take over the lower level routine jobs, the digital economy is already creating demand for highly skilled professionals. According to a BCG study, already in US and German companies, there is a shortage of qualified professionals which is hampering their shift towards complete digital transformation. A Gartner study too forecasts that one-third of all jobs in the technology sectors will go unfulfilled by 2020 due to talent constraints.

Around the world, many employers complain about their inability to fill job vacancies. In Europe, roughly 4 out of 10 establishments report difficulties in finding workers with the required skills. In India, about 60 per cent employers are particularly affected by skill deficits. Skill gaps usually reported by employers around the globe include a lack of generic or soft skills, namely, teamwork, interpersonal skills, leadership, knowledge of foreign languages, readiness to learn, problem-solving and IT skills [4].

Perhaps that's why some universities around the world now offer majors in programmes that didn't even exist five years ago, such as robotics engineering, game design, cybersecurity, online journalism, human-computer interaction, e-business/e-commerce and data science. Also take a look at job titles such as android developer, the Zumba instructor, social media intern, the data scientist, user interface (UI) and user experience (UX) designer, cloud services specialist, the big data architect, etc., which did not exist five years ago [5]. There has to be a paradigm shift from spinning degrees or degree holders to producing precision, integrated and knowledge workers; those who can build challenges around themselves, are self-motivated and have the capability to acquire appropriate knowledge, skill sets required for a task, finding solutions to newer problems and upward scaling.

Johnson Graduate School of Management at Cornell University has launched a new curriculum which prepares students in a two-year MBA programme to lead, with emphasis on critical thinking, target leadership skills, analyse data and model through experiential or immersive learning.

Shifting Geopolitical and Economic Power

This thought connects to the wage disparity and economic growth rates, multiple power centres, depletion of resources, massive migration to urban areas and the rise by the middle class in most developing countries, etc.

Since the Second World War, the United States had occupied the mantle of global economic leadership. The shift in this global economic order is taking place with the slow demise of the United States and the rise of China as the global economic power, followed by India. A shifting of realignment in economic relationship is taking place, such as China's One Belt One Road economic platform. These complex ever-changing relationships between nations and group of nations, such as the emergence of Asian Economic Community, will write new rules for doing business globally.

The realignment of global economic order is bringing about certain fundamental changes. The US dollar which rules the world market since the Second World War is losing its dominance, and no single currency will be able to replace it in the foreseeable future. The global financial institutions such as the World Bank and IMF which were led by the United States are also losing their power and being challenged by the emergence of new global institutions such as Asian Infrastructure Investment Bank. China is increasingly muscling its way into domains which were once the exclusive turf of Western economies. Its rapid move into this role has given it enormous leverage in developing and influencing trade networks such as One Belt One Road initiative.

WTO is diminishing in stature and increasingly replaced by bilateral and regional trade bodies. The trade shift and imbalance are being witnessed. China has capitalized upon its international competitiveness and learnt a lesson very early that the first mover advantage in being a manufacturing-based economy and as an international supplier will emerge as its core competence. It has started reaping and it has become a specialist in developing cluster-based specialized manufacturing set-ups around the country, difficult to compete by any standards.

In this interconnected world, talent is now moving where it is needed most worldwide. Many agreements are being hammered out between nations allowing easy movement of talent. One is not restricted by national boundaries but can seek scarce talent wherever available. Likewise, many international companies are moving their R&D centres to countries where such talent is easily available such as India. This provides opportunities for both leaders to seek talent and talent to seek place of work worldwide.

Technology too is playing disruptive part in distributing the traditional source of geopolitical power and stability. Mobile payment technologies are most advanced in countries like Kenya in Africa where a large part of the population has no access to traditional banking system. Blockchain, a technology for automatic verification of ledgers and the backbone of digital currencies like Bitcoin, will be increasingly deployed in banking and financial institutions, undermining the powerful status of large monolithic Western banking companies. Today, 'game changer' can originate anywhere and this unpredictability is also creating ripples in long established institutions. Today, the leader in mobile banking is Kenya, a poor developing nation. As a business leader, how can you manage this complexity? How can you cross the threshold to the next economic order with confidence and skill?

Diversity and Inclusion

These lay an emphasis on multiculturalism, the racial and ethnic diversity we encounter, the gender equality and the economic development that should be equitable, etc.

Too often, we think that diversity and inclusion are not considered as vital assets towards organizational performance. On the contrary, we consider them being confined with the HR department. They are often visualized as just token programmes and not key ingredients for the long-term vitality and success of an organization, particularly in the areas of leadership development and growth.

Workplace at enterprises is moving away from the straitjacketed line and staff models to flatter and loosely structured organizations. In such scenarios, the role of leadership is also changing. Enterprises are realizing that inclusion and diversity are not just politically correct slogans but are essential to business and cultivating strong leaders. The flat organizations with evolved distributed decision-making are quick to respond changing external stimuli. Leadership resides at all levels as teams are empowered to attain organizational goals. Within this environment, leading is about distributed or collaborative leadership, understanding internal networks which means a more evolved humbler leader who accepts that he/she does not have all the answers and is an enabler of work environment where teams excel.

Originally, as considered by researchers, diversity is referred to race, gender or orientation. However, currently the meaning has expanded. Diversity, increasingly seen as an organizational asset, also encompasses economic, educational and generational differences, besides other disparities in the background. Thereby, accepting diversity and inclusion within the organization framework implies additional training, especially towards developing a strategic and distinct outlook.

Diversity's counterpart, which is inclusion, emphasizes that in an organization, all individuals are valuable, not just those who are 'different'. This concept of inclusion confers greater importance to candid opinions, talents and the skills possessed by its team members.

Both diversity and inclusion are potential tools towards inculcating leadership, especially in flatter organizations, since their combined effect is on risk-taking propensity. A lesser hierarchical system demands its members to self-govern, self-lead and mutually submit to the leadership [6].

Individualism and Entrepreneurship
These examine and refer to the freelance work versus the employee loyalty, their risk-taking and level of entrepreneur spirit, their multidisciplinary pursuits, renting of talent followed by freelancing and individual aspirations in life.

Independence is becoming the dominant motivator for a large section of the population, particularly for millennials. They don't want to be micromanaged. Outside of the workplace, empowered by digital platforms and ecosystems, many are choosing entrepreneurship and self-employment over traditional corporate employment. Many top graduates from IITs and IIMs are opting for start-ups rather than big salary tags. New Age individuals have independent dreams and have latent desire to build castles around it. They have become more passionate and expressive with a deluge of creative ideas ready to be explored.

There is a change taking place in the working life of corporate professionals and managers. Many, especially those who have made a secured financial future due to smart savings, are ready to take a break from their jobs to pursue further education and even become volunteers with NGOs or become freelancers. Many also nurse ambitions to become entrepreneurs. A study has predicted that at least 50 per cent of the workforce will be made up of freelancers by 2020. As organizations begin to rent rather than hire talent, they will have to make do with a lower level of commitment. They will need to create career paths and roles to serve the entrepreneurial aspirations of the highly skilled talent they seek.

Well-being and Purpose

This is the desire for personal, social and the communal impact one can exhibit, a pure reflection of self and the purpose, the expression, appreciation and respect, the importance of physical and mental health balance.

Leaders are increasingly turning their attention to the millennial generation, whose attitudes and preferences may profoundly reshape workplaces and society. Like those in every generation before them, millennials strive for a life well lived. Besides regular salaries and benefits, they also want to be engaged in those jobs, meaning they are emotionally and behaviourally connected to them.

In addition to finding steady, engaging jobs, millennials want to have high levels of well-being, which means more than being physically fit. Yes, millennials want to be healthy, but they also want a purposeful life, active community and social ties and financial stability. Regarding that financial stability, millennials want to be able to spend money on what they want—not just on what they need.

Harvard Professor Howard Gardner in his book *Five Minds for the Future* had already anticipated these trends a decade back and has offered a road map for people to be future-ready for any job or career, even those which may not exist today. In the future, people will need to have these minds that are very disciplined, capable of synthesizing information, being creative, respectful and ethical in all respects. These five minds are based on Professor Gardner's critical analysis of what is required for today and in future. These different minds refer to critical thinking, using one's mind judiciously, the ability to uncover real problem followed by finding innovative solutions and so on. The latter two minds, the respectful and the ethical ones, are concerned in dealing with other people, with the world as we encounter it continuously. These, in particular, have to do more with the character than with IQ or intelligence [7].

There is definitely a hierarchy towards developing these five different minds. A certain discipline is required in developing critical ways of thinking before one can synthesize this acquired knowledge. It is understood that one cannot be creative unless there is some discipline followed by synthesizing.

Similarly, when he talks about respect, Professor Gardner is referring to about how people treat one another. In most organizations, we still treat people as infants and micromanage their output, have large bound manuals for their conduct, communication is one way with instructions downwards and the higher-ups are the fountainhead of all knowledge. We have to treat people as adults who can think and plan for themselves. Ethics has to do with questioning our role in the society. Are we responsible members of the society in which we live as well as the world we inhabit?

These are the different kinds of minds that need to be developed, both for surviving and in perceiving the world where one desires to live in. Ideally, we could have a world that endows creativity, but if people intend to be disrespectful and unethical, we will end up again as another Enron or Lehman Brothers. Why don't we encourage in having a world whereby people are disciplined and intuitive in acquiring knowledge? But if there is an inability to synthesize the information, the world will drown them leaving no scope to survive.

We are already viewing the early effects of these megatrends. With the IT industry vertically shifting in its nature of work due to increased use of digital technology, a leading firm has realized that the majority of the workforce cannot imbibe the required rapid and emerging skill sets; thus, it has cautioned that increased job losses at the middle and senior levels are bound to happen.

'I am not very pessimistic, but it is a challenging task and intends to believe that 60-65 percent of them are just not trainable', Capgemini India's CEO Srinivas Kandula said. These observations came in after NASSCOM pointed out on the need to retrain around 1.5 million people, very near to half of the sectoral workforce. This has been as a result of changing nature of work with newer technologies coming in practice. These critical remarks have come across post a study that stated that around 80 per cent engineering graduates were found to be unemployable [8].

According to another study by employability assessment company Aspiring Minds, only 4.77 per cent candidates in India can write the correct logic for a programme—a minimum requirement for any programming job. 'Lack of programming skills is adversely impacting the IT and data science ecosystem in India ... India needs to catch up' [9].

This is the state of IT industry which has been called a sunrise industry. The days of hiring in thousands seem to be coming towards an end for the $155 billion Indian IT industry, and all indicators show that bulk recruitment is now being rapidly replaced by niche intake. The industry, which attracted technical talent in droves with thousands of engineering graduates, many from low-grade institutions, lapped up by companies, is now focused on just-in-time hiring or of people demonstrating special skills. This is also apparent in hundreds of poorly equipped engineering colleges being asked to close down by the All India Council for Technical Education (AICTE) because of plunging admissions.

The news coming out of other industries such as manufacturing is not very encouraging. India is looking at a jobless GDP growth unless drastic changes are made in the country's educational system, from primary to PhD.

However, untrainable does not mean 'unlearnable'. We know of at least two persons, both BSc from run-of-the-mill colleges, who trained themselves to positions of senior management.

One of them came to my (Suhayl Abidi) attention when he was teaching MS Word, Excel in an evening tutorial class. I found him willing to learn and provided a contract job in data entry under me and introduced him to IT professionals in my place of work, a large refinery. He learnt and saved a large sum of money for the company by developing an in-house supply chain management programme. Today, he is the deputy head of the supply chain function.

The other too, a BSc, was employed by me in another company, on contract, to scan over half million pages of documents to digital format, a purely mechanical repetitive work. I again found him willing and able to learn programming on his own and provided support through books and networking with IT professionals. He later moved as the head of IT backend for a UK-based drugs marketing company, working in both England and India. Today, he is a successful entrepreneur.

Most of the workers in IT industry, who are staring at possible job losses, are certainly better educated, trained and experienced than these two.

In contrast to these two, some other IT professionals I know never tried to upgrade their knowledge and skills level once they were placed in body shopping jobs with leading Indian companies, going abroad for onsite work. They did make some money. However, their skills level is the same as it was when they joined, despite many opportunities available to learn online today. They are at risk of losing their jobs.

Not only regular jobs are being lost, many jobs, which were performed by full-time employees, are moving to contract and flexi employees. This is both a threat and an opportunity in waiting for those who are alert to changing work scenarios.

Visualize the Work Scenario Tomorrow

Automation in order giving and food delivery in fast food restaurants such as McDonald's would do away with many front-line jobs. Only kitchen jobs may remain for a little longer duration. Finally, even these will go. For example, a company in San Francisco that's working on a hamburger robot that can crank out about 400 hamburgers an hour.

At a fibre-spinning mill in a company where I worked, workers who replaced full bobbins with empty ones were replaced by automatic transport of roving bobbins robots whenever a sensor gave signal of a full bobbin. Eighty jobs were lost. In the same plant, automation at warehousing replaced nearly 400 workers.

In a plant under construction in the United States, production lines manned by the Sewbot will be capable of making 1.2 million T-shirts (the largest produced clothing in the garment industry) a year—and the effects of automation will be felt in garment factories in the developing world, including India, over the next decade as the cost of automation comes down.

Similarly, cash counters in supermarkets are likely to disappear. This coming transformation in the way you pay for items in bricks-and-mortar stores will occur through a network of sensors placed strategically around stores, which will enable retailers to recognize you (through your smartphone or other devices) when you walk through the door. Inexpensive sensors also will be attached to (or embedded in) items available for purchase. And the stores will already have your preferred payment information on file, so when you exit the store with your chosen merchandise, you'll simply be billed automatically, totally skipping any traditional checkout experience.

Many restaurants are already in the vanguard of transforming the checkout experience. A growing number of restaurants are using iPods or other tablets to have diners place their own orders and then check themselves out at the end of the meal. Green shoots are also being seen in India with the opening of the first waiter-less restaurant in Chennai where orders are placed on an iPod and delivered by robots. China alone has over 2,000 such restaurants. If such a change becomes widespread, the implications for waitstaff employment will be profound.

If you think your white-collar job is safe, think again. For example, BlackRock, world's largest asset manager is replacing portfolio managers with AI in stock picking. A new study by consulting firm PwC says nearly 40 per cent of American jobs are at risk of being automated by the early 2030s. A PwC partner says automation could next hit insurance underwriters and agents, and financial advisors.

Crowdsourcing and Contract, and Job-specific Platforms

Some work will become more task oriented, with more work available through crowdsourcing and job-specific platforms, and will free many people to branch out on their own such as Uber and Ola drivers.

Crowdsourcing is becoming the new place for leveraging your talent as a service. Amazon Mechanical Turk (MTurk) is a crowdsourcing Internet marketplace which brings those who need work and others who want work done to seek each other. It is one of the sites of Amazon Web Services. Employers or 'requesters' can post jobs known as human intelligence tasks (HITs), such as writing product descriptions, cleaning or verifying data, etc. Workers called 'providers' can then browse among existing jobs and complete them in exchange for a monetary payment set by the employer.

Crowdsourcing communities such as Kaggle and InnoCentive allow companies to attract talent without much upfront investment. They can utilize specific talent for a particular project. Freelancers are well connected with their peer groups and have up-to-date skills. Kaggle, for example, is a platform for predictive modelling and analytics competitions on which companies and researchers post their data, and statisticians and data miners from all over the world compete to produce the best models. Data scientists can also test their skills using the tutorials available. US insurance company Allstate regularly hosts competitions on Kaggle to solve business problems. At one such competition, freelancers' claims prediction rate was 271 per cent more accurate than internal models.

InnoCentive, another crowdsourcing platform, describes itself as the 'world's first open innovation marketplace'. Its motto is a problem shared is a problem solved. Companies, which InnoCentive calls 'seekers', post their challenges on the firm's website. 'Solvers' compete to win cash 'prizes' offered by the seekers. Over 150 companies, even large ones such as Procter & Gamble and The Dow Chemical Company have benefitted from posting their challenges. A recent innovation called InnoCentive@Work allows challenges to be first offered to companies' own employees.

As against Blackrock, WorldQuant is a quantitative hedge fund that manages more than $4.5 billion in assets.

It develops and deploys systematic financial strategies across a variety of asset classes in global markets, utilizing a proprietary research platform and risk management process. Its 600 full-time employees identify recurring patterns to boost returns. Even here, this company which employs over 120 PhDs has to seek talent among the freelancer world and was the first to sponsor a competition for coding with potential offer of part-time work. One such winner was Indian Institute of Technology, Mumbai, student Gangwar.

Gangwar is a quantitative analyst or, in financial jargon, a quant, a person who specializes in the application of mathematical and statistical methods—such as numerical or quantitative techniques—to financial and risk management problems. He entered the competition in 2014 and ranked in the top 50 among more than 5,000 contestants, and in that year earned $7,000 working for WorldQuant as a consultant.

The 22-year-old logs onto a website connecting him to his boss in Greenwich, Connecticut, USA, and begins tinkering with models for souping up strategies at one of the world's largest quant firms. Gangwar has everything WorldQuant could want—extreme computer literacy, enough hardware to dial in from 8,000 miles away, ambition—without a Wall Street professional's demands on pay. That's not to say there wasn't a steep learning curve.

'It was hard at the start', said Gangwar, whose coding skills over two months of competing in the WorldQuant Challenge were good enough to land him a part-time job. 'I had little knowledge in finance, so I had to Google a lot to learn the different terminologies' [10].

Crowdsourcing part-time quants as a way to find workers have become a full-blown craze on Wall Street in the past year. As active managers fight chronic underperformance and revulsion over their fees, funds are looking for ways to cut costs when it comes to talent.

Gangwar has now quit his mining engineering course and has opted for another part-time course to focus on quant. He and his two friends have pooled their resources to build a similar software backbone to launch their own quant hedge fund for the Indian equity market.

Gangwar is the kind of person who will survive and prosper, whatever the future has in store for him, as he is continuously scanning the environment, spotting opportunities and continuously learning to be on top.

Increased Flexibility

In the Industrial Age, work was restricted to 'set-time, set-place' barriers. Workers had to reach a fixed place, an office or factory, at the same time to get the work done. Today, technology such as mobile, video conferencing, cloud-based document sharing and online collaboration has broken through those barriers. Even office layout is now changing where there is no fixed place for a worker to sit and work and you have to seek a vacant desk, connect your laptop and start working. The office, as we perceive, is going obsolete. By 2020, it's projected that one in three workers will be working online.

An actuarial professional I (Abidi) know works full time from home in Boston for one of the largest insurance companies in the United States. Another professional works full time from home in Mumbai selling database services for one of the largest IT companies in the world to clients in North America through video conferencing. Businesses that ignore this reality—and the benefits it entails—will find themselves left behind.

In today's context, virtual arrangements from remote locations have emerged to be a common practice. Currently, according to one study, many firms reported with over 30 per cent of mid to senior level global respondents had worked three or more days in a week from remote locations. Yet another half of them did so with at least two days in a week. A recent research by the WorldatWork acknowledges that nearly 88 per cent of organizations does offer formal telework arrangements.

The success of remote working mandates a higher degree of trust as the managers need to empower workers as they can no longer supervise closely.

The study also evinced yet another fact that one of the most effective ways in building this trust is in providing people with some tools, skills and the required resources to succeed. Providing an ongoing access to such learning opportunities not only prepares the workforce to perform effectively but, at the same time, also increases their sense of connection and the willingness to contribute towards organizational objectives [11].

Today's workplace is a virtual and/or physical environment, characterized by connections, collaboration and user choice that enables the worker to be more agile and perform activities anywhere, anytime.

Many workers already work from coffee shops such as Café Coffee Day and food courts in malls. Many individuals, groups and teams are increasingly meeting in such central places rather than move to their office in distant places. This not only adds an element of social interaction to offset the potential isolation of working from home but also creates communities of professionals who can collaborate and network together. Some companies such as the new offices of drug maker GlaxoSmithKline at Philadelphia are also moving towards the connected workplace by doing away with assigned workspaces. By using unassigned seating and seeing the workplaces as a connected environment, employees can work anywhere in the building with those that are directly needed for any given assignment.

Such changes are multiplying the informal learning opportunities available to employees.

To summarize, there are many reasons to be hopeful.

New disruptive technologies will certainly make certain human interventions obsolete but history has shown that technological advancements create more jobs than they displace. We have to adapt to changing scenarios by putting humans in places which can take advantages of unique human capabilities. Technology will allow us to redeploy people from the drudgery of low-level repeatable jobs to lead a more socially meaningful life. We are at an inflection point where the policymakers have to make a choice. Continue producing unemployable workforce or do a radical change in our education system from primary to tertiary. We have to make education our topmost priority just as tiny Vietnam has done.

This does not mean that we should overlook the concerns these changes will bring. Today, blue-collar workers are threatened but slowly the innovations in technology will start threatening the white-collar workers too. The country's skills mission has largely failed and our policymakers have not yet fully realized the paradigm shift that is taking place. Tinkering with skills or vocational programmes at intermediate levels will not work unless the primary and secondary education produces workers who can be reskilled or retrained. Quality must start from primary schools itself.

Call centres is one such white-collar job sector which employs half a million people in India, which will see job losses in future due to emergence of technologies such as chatbot.

To start looking which jobs will flourish and which will go, let us first examine how leading companies such as Google are realigning their hiring strategies.

And who was Google hiring? Laszlo Bock, a senior VP of people operations for Google, elucidates. 'We were biased toward people with fancy degrees.... If you attend Harvard versus being number one at SUNY Binghamton, who does better?' He further stated that the best students from any school outperformed the average students from major Ivy League universities. Bock commented, 'So there's actually an evidence to suggest [that] as a recruiter, you're better off casting a wider net, which is what we do.' This is definitely an eye-opener for all Indian recruiters, who are willing to pay phenomenal starting salaries to the graduates from top management schools. Introspection is required!

Bock says that it is an assessment that the grades too are overrated.

> After analysis, it was found that these grades have a small predictive nature for the first set of years, but for the rest of life do not matter at all... What matters is the education you got and your learning ability ... We know those things are predictive.

Google's focus has also shifted away from being influenced by SAT scores. He said it had been a mistake for the company to be asking all candidates, irrespective of the age, for their SAT scores (college transcript), often passing on those that didn't score high enough [12].

Hiring algorithms may objectively match skill sets with job opportunities. Whichever way you look, the future worker will be a thinking and continuously learning worker. The routine mundane jobs will be either automated or pay very little with few avenues of advancement. Not so long ago, thinking was the domain of top management, led by the CEO or managing director. This team of experienced and successful leaders and managers were considered the fountain of knowledge from which distilled instructions were conveyed to the rank and file who were supposed to perform their work in a limited sphere. Today, knowledge is widespread and leaders would have to work with people who may know more than themselves.

Learning in the past was limited to print media and occasional meetings and conferences. Today learning is everywhere and informal learning is happening all the time through blogs, Wikis, Twitter, Facebook and other social media sites, broadcasting sites, YouTube, interactive digital sources and many others innumerable ever-expanding universe.

Organizational Structure Redesign

To enhance competitiveness, effectively manage core business processes and maintain flexibility, organizations have flattened their structures, eliminated layers of management and are utilizing teams.

Flatter structures allow more interaction and networking between people working in various parts of the organization, reduces customer response time, allows the evolution of empowered employee and establishes an inspiring culture. As skills and competencies continue to evolve, teams can be structured in a number of ways as situation and work demand.

This enables organizations to be flexible and respond rapidly to changing business requirements and customer needs. Project teams are producing better, cheaper and faster results than the traditional hierarchal management structures. It also enables employees to build on their skills as they develop their experience through each new project. They are continually re-skilling and upskilling.

The need to cut operating costs and streamline operations is resulting in practically everything that is not strategic being outsourced.

Contract or temporary workers were at one time solely restricted to low-skilled work. However, today specialized temporary workers are outsourced in highly skilled areas such as finance, IT, sales and marketing, etc. Even CEOs are outsourced for turning around sick companies or when a right person is not available to the satisfaction of the Board. Such interim CEO joins for a limited tenure and leaves after the job is over. After Satyam Computer Services scandal blew up, the government-appointed interim board appointed A. S. Murty as CEO whose tenure ended when the company was sold to Tech Mahindra.

Increasingly, professionally qualified people are being brought into organizations on contract to complete specific projects. This provides management with greater flexibility to deploy resources, when and where required.

A new study, 'Millennials and the Future of Work', conducted by independent research firm Genesis Research Associates examined perspectives on the future of work. Professionals are today crafting entrepreneurial, independent paths to freedom. The conclusions were as follows:

1. Seventy-two per cent of those still at 'regular' jobs want to quit, to be entirely independent; 61 per cent say they likely will within two years.
2. Freedom is the top reason those at 'regular' jobs would like to quit; and 89 per cent say they prefer to work when and where they choose (versus in a corporate, 9–5 job).
3. Sixty-nine per cent want to work on projects, which interest them.

4. Today, 90 per cent of independent workers think entrepreneurship reflects having a certain mindset rather than one starting an enterprise. When asked to define an entrepreneur, aspects of this mindset mentioned included being a 'self-starter', 'risk-taker', 'visionary' and someone who 'spots an opportunity' [13].

Companies are increasingly hiring knowledge workers to their workforce who work on demand, are flexible in response to fluctuating needs and move towards leaner, nimbler companies that can survive and prosper in the rapidly changing marketplace. In addition, people would change their workplace more often. The loyalty of employee is transferring from organization to profession. A software professional is more likely to share knowledge with his online group, which reciprocates his knowledge sharing rather than the organization he works for and where he is shackled by line and staff, and other organizational constraints in knowledge sharing.

Jobs of the Future

According to MIT Professor Erik Brynjolfsson, despite AI and robotics making routine-processing tasks fast and cheaper, there shall also be a surge in job growth in fields such as nursing, sales, etc. These are jobs requiring interpersonal, creative and entrepreneurial skills. Brynjolfsson has observed that like the Industrial Revolution having accelerated economic growth and newer ways to work, this next wave of technology will definitely seed newer career opportunities. Specialists, the creative class and people who have jobs that require emotional intelligence (EI) such as salespeople, coaches, customer service specialists and people who create everything from writing and art to new products, platforms and services will always find opportunities in future. Jobs in health care, personal services and other areas that are tough to automate will also remain in demand, as will trade skills and science, technology and mathematics [14].

It does not matter what is the level of pay. A radiologist reading images and consequently reporting is a highly paid and sought-after career. However, there is more likelihood of him being replaced by automation than that of a general practitioner. Workers will need to engage in lifelong education to remain on top of how job and career trends are shifting to remain viable in an ever-changing workplace.

Professor Brynjolfsson's advice for those joining the job market is: there are jobs that machines are substitutes for, jobs that machines are complements for and jobs that machines don't affect at all. Your strategy should be to stay far, far away from things that machines are substitutes for, like routine information processing.

Another strategy of looking for jobs is where machines and men and complementary. As servers become more powerful and cheaper, these can now store huge amount of data, originated from, for example, IoT. With such proliferation of online and cloud-based databases, there would be a serious shortage of skilled professionals such as data scientists.

The third interesting category is on those skills which machines would not affect much. We shall witness employment growth in jobs requiring nurturing and caring, interpersonal skills, etc. Machines cannot be substitutes where behaviour precedes and that they are not the complements for jobs such as nursing, teaching, sales, leadership and coaching. So there is some hedging on these kind of jobs for the time being. Learning creativity, interpersonal skills, entrepreneurship and teamwork will be more important in future than any degree from a top school. These survival skills also include creative thinking and will be discussed in detail later in the book. However, one thing is clear, those who create, manage and decipher knowledge in any form will comprise the workforce of the future.

Thus, we need to be prepared with enhanced skills, honed each day, where technology dominates and is undergoing a rapid change for the next 10 or 20 years. This implies that we start moving away from rote teaching and move towards building curriculum which encourages creativity, entrepreneurship and interpersonal skills.

Rote learning will not disappear from our educational system in the near future, so the onus is on the generation next to complement their education with new knowledge skills for the future. This is as true for the student who is applying for his/her first job as for CEO of a company. Experiential learning will dominate. Those who have the power to ingress knowledge timely in whatever form it comes, be it explicit but mostly tacit, will scale to newer heights. There will be a phenomenon on reverse learning. The New Age learner will teach the elderly generations, peer groups and superiors better, newer dimensions, more effective and precise methods to solve problems and generate multiple solutions in a knowledge-based economy. This is going to be the future of work.

References

1. Sood, Varun. 2016, 7 June. Wipro to Deploy AI Platform Holmes to Do the Job of 3,000 Engineers. *LiveMint.* Available at http://www.livemint.com/Companies/wnAH NojuGO2En8zQpItZLP/Wipro-to-deploy-AI-platform-Holmes-to-do-the-job-of-3000-en.html (accessed 6 February 2018).
2. Bhalla, Vikram, Susanne Dyrchs and Rainer Strack. 2017, 27 March. *Twelve Forces That Will Radically Change How Organizations Work.* Boston Consulting Group. Available at https://www.bcg.com/publications/2017/people-organization-strategy-twelve-forces-radically-change-organizations-work.aspx (accessed 6 February 2018).
3. Mitchinson, Adam and Robert Morris. 2014. *Learning About Learning Agility.* Center for Creative Leadership. Available at https://www.ccl.org/wp-content/uploads/2015/04/LearningAgility.pdf (accessed 6 February 2018).
4. World Economic Forum. 2014, January. *Matching Skills and Labour Market Needs: Building Social Partnerships for Better Skills and Better Jobs.* Available at http://www3.weforum.org/docs/GAC/2014/WEF_GAC_Employment_MatchingSkillsLabourMarket_Report_2014.pdf (accessed 6 February 2018).
5. Murthy, Sohan. 2014, 6 January. *Top 10 Job Titles That Didn't Exist 5 Years Ago.* LinkedIn. Available at https://business.linkedin.com/talent-solutions/blog/2014/01/top-10-job-titles-that-didnt-exist-5-years-ago-infographic (accessed 6 February 2018).

6. Tavakoli, Mahan. 2015, May. Diversity and Inclusion Drive Success for Today's Leaders. *TD Magazine*. Available at https://www.td.org/magazines/td-magazine/diversity-and-inclusion-drive-success-for-todays-leaders (accessed 6 February 2018).

7. Gardner, Howard. 2004. *Five Minds for the Future*. Brighton, MA: Harvard Business School Press.

8. Press Trust of India. 2017, 19 February. Capgemini India Chief Says 65% of IT Employees Not Retrainable. *The Times of India*. Available at https://timesofindia.indiatimes.com/toi-features/business/capgemini-india-chief-says-65-of-it-employees-not-retrainable/articleshow/57232478.cms (accessed 6 February 2018).

9. Press Trust of India. 2017, 20 April. 95% Engineers in India Unfit for Programming Jobs: Study. *LiveMint*. Available at http://www.livemint.com/Industry/cFUpp8wN9sXhXBVaBXRHlM/95-engineers-in-India-unfit-for-software-development-jobs.html (accessed 6 February 2018).

10. Burger, Dani. 2017, 17 March. WorldQuant's Hunger Gamers are the Low-cost Alternative to PhDs. *LiveMint*. Available at http://www.livemint.com/Industry/gMOX36FczIDMzuTKC1pCLJ/WorldQuants-hunger-gamers-are-the-lowcost-alternative-to-P.html (accessed 6 February 2018).

11. Smith, Aaron and Janna Anderson. 2014, 6 August. *AI, Robotics, and the Future of Jobs*. Pew Research Center. Available at http://www.pewinternet.org/2014/08/06/future-of-jobs/ (accessed 6 February 2018).

12. The Wharton School of the University of Pennsylvania. 2016, 26 February. Open Sourcing Google's HR Secrets. *Knowledge@Wharton*. Available at http://knowledge.wharton.upenn.edu/article/open-sourcing-googles-hr-secrets/ (accessed 6 February 2018).

13. Schawbel, Dan. 2013, 22 May. *Millennials and the Future of Work*. Available at http://millennialbranding. com/2013/millennials-future-work-study/ (accessed 6 February 2018).
14. Brynjolfsson, Erik. 2015, April. How to Outsmart the Robots in the Next Hiring Boom. *Wired*. Available at https://www.wired.com/brandlab/2015/04/erik-brynjolfsson-outsmart-robots-next-hiring-boom/ (accessed 6 February 2018).

Chapter 4
Who Will Win: Preparing for the Future

We have met the enemy and he is us.

—Pogo the cartoon character

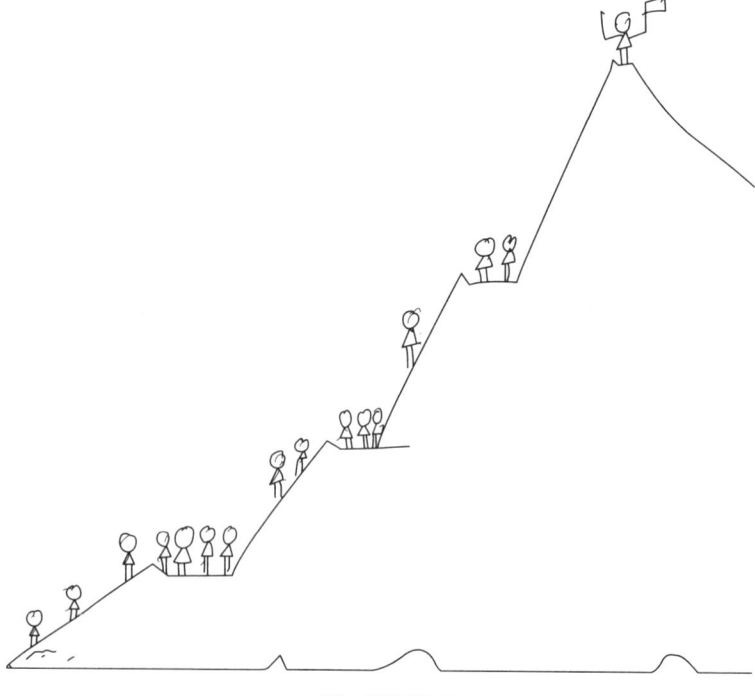

Who Will Win?

Each year, thousands leave college and university campuses in droves, and thousands more are on the move for a career change, either voluntarily or through voluntary retirement scheme (VRS), at all levels of the hierarchy. There is an opportunity to relearn new careers where competition hasn't reached critical mass. There are thousands of jobs which were only created in the last decade, for example, mobile application developer, data miner, educational counsellors (to help ease the process of interviewing and testing in schools from preschool to college), social media managers, psychological experts in organizations, cloud computing services, eldercare, sustainability experts, etc. Even theoretical subject such as mathematics, for which, at one time, teaching was the only option, is today a highly sought-after qualification in actuarial, automation and software development.

We have to look for wider application of our education and skills. For example, a not so glamorous degree such as library science can become a hot degree right now as these graduates are trained in managing large amount of data and can move into a new hot area such as data mining.

Do you know what the reality is? We are living in times where excessive disruption at the workplace will reduce, at times, our ability to see the future. The safe job you were banking upon has disappeared. There is a complete change in workplace dynamics.

According to Farai Chideya, author of *The Episodic Career*, whether we work for ourselves, a small company or a large enterprise, we're in an era of disruption and psychological self-employment. We all must think about retraining ourselves in case our jobs or industries change radically and advocate for our own long-term economic health. The great recession may be over, but the period of intense disruption and creation in the world of jobs and careers will go on for the foreseeable future. We are already seeing a lot of churning in the IT field. Alibaba's Chairman Jack Ma warned 'that society could see decades of pain thanks to the disruption caused by the internet and new technologies to different areas of the economy'. Speaking about potential job disruptions caused by technology, Ma said, 'In the coming 30 years, the world's pain will be much more than happiness, because there are many more problems that we have come across' [1]. Even when you reach the top, there is no certainty of a job. The tenure of a CEO is getting shorter and nobody knows it better than Cyrus Mistry who was ousted overnight from the post of Chairman of Tata Sons and his tenure lasted less than four years. This was an incredibly unexpected decision by an Indian corporate.

Nobody knows what's going to happen, but at the end you've got to be prepared to take care of yourself.

The first step is knowledge about self. Everyone possesses the ability to use a variety of skills you have within you. Who says you only have to use one skillset in your career? 'You're not just the job you have now or the job you had five years ago, you're a compilation of skills and assets, which can be used in many contexts' [2].

People with life experience have skills, talents and abilities that other people don't. First is to know what generic knowledge or skills asset you have. Many of us do volunteer activities or join NGOs to fulfil our role as responsible members of the society or have hobbies through which we can leverage certain skills. Many times, we are stuck in a job because we do not know what else we can do.

Almost 15 years back, when I (Abidi) was working in a human relations function in a pharmaceutical company, the president of my human resources group assigned me the job of finding a mid-level executive who can work as No. 2 in a new department the company had created. This was business development where you obtain licences of drugs from patent holders worldwide for manufacture and sale in India. The days of copycat drug development were over and licensing was one way forward. This required multidisciplinary knowledge of worldwide drug development scenario, estimating market potential, intellectual property laws, especially dealing with licensing and soft skills such as communication and negotiation. All that in one person! There were no such individuals in the company or even in the entire industry as our company was the first to have this function. After scouting for more than a month and interviewing many candidates, I zeroed in on Deepak (name changed), a middle-level marketing manager with about seven years of experience. This was a lateral shift and no promotion was promised, though it did come at a later stage. Every one of Deepak's colleagues and his bosses advised him not to join as he will lose seven years of valuable marketing experience.

I advised him that marketing is a crowded field, littered with managers with higher qualifications such as MBA. Deepak never acquired an MBA and now he was getting left out of the race for senior positions. This weighed heavily on him and he felt inadequate. I suggested that he had many other skills and competencies which are essential for business development and he should make this lateral move. By the time other companies wake up to creating such functions, he would already have acquired valuable experience.

On my advice, he took up this new career move and stayed for three years learning on the job. Meanwhile, looking at the success of this function, other companies too wanted such professionals but there were none around except Deepak and he started getting calls from major companies. Ultimately, he joined a multinational drug company, worked there for two years at Mumbai and then the company posted him to Singapore with a bigger responsibility for several countries. Today, he is working as business development director at one of the world's largest medical devices company, working out of Dubai. He is way ahead of his colleagues, not only in monetary terms but also level and responsibility by many years. His need for an MBA has long gone into oblivion.

What went right with Deepak? He took the risk, moved early to a career of the future with less competition, gained new knowledge and learnt many new skills, largely on his own. Among other competencies, his business acumen was sharpened through roles in strategic planning, business development, new products planning, alliance management, and mergers and acquisitions. He was ready for the big jump when the market for such professionals got hot. He realized early that more than education and experience, it is self-awareness, letting go of old and continuous learning is what counts today. Today, these zigzagging career paths are becoming more common.

Definitely, not all have to abandon the traditional course of action. If one is ambitiously working towards for a potentially achievable goal, such as managing a division, disruption may be not required. This is what Clayton M. Christensen, father of disruptive innovation and author of *The Innovator's Dilemma*, terms sustaining innovation, a phenomenon when a company gets better every day at what it's already doing while providing additional value to its existing customers. Generally, in mid career, you reach a plateau or find that you are not cut out for further growth or that you don't want to continue climbing the same ladder, it is time that you should disrupt yourself as Deepak did. Companies which are good at survival do the same.

According to Christensen's research on disruptive innovation, when a company religiously pursues growth in a new market rather than in an established one, the odds of success are six times higher and thus the revenue potential is also 20 times greater. Although it is impossible to quantify the effects of career disruption for a person but can yield similar results, as we have seen in the case of Deepak. Current stakeholders in your company will probably discourage you towards disruption since foresight is rare. For most of us, holding steady implies slipping—as we ignore the threat of competition from younger, more agile innovators, bypass opportunities for greater reward and sacrifice personal growth [3].

Therefore, you must set out to disrupt your career, just as Deepak did, before it is forced upon you. For that, you must seek out your disruptive strength. The process starts with knowing yourself.

Self-awareness

Self-awareness is generally defined as conscious knowledge of one's own character and feelings. We look back and reflect on our past actions and evaluate our behaviour with or without the feedback of others we trust. As Mahatma Gandhi said, 'Our greatness lies not so much in being able to remake the world as being able to remake ourselves.' We actively seek to know about ourselves and our weaknesses such as anger, procrastination and impulsiveness and make attempts to improve ourselves with or without the help of others. Without reflection, we do ourselves a disservice by blaming others for our maladaptive behaviour and continue our path of downward spiral of self-destruction. Taking responsibility for our actions is the first step in changing for improvement.

Sharon Merriman from the University of Georgia, Athens, has described the self-aware adult learner as one who:

1. has an independent self-concept;
2. can direct his/her own learning;
3. has accumulated a reservoir of life experiences that can be a resource;
4. has learning needs closely related to changing social roles;

5. is problem centred and interested in the immediate application of knowledge and
6. is internally motivated, rather than externally, to learn.

Thus, without skills towards self-awareness, thinking can be distorted by a self-deception, a thought process that can lead someone to be misinformed and cause them to miscommunicate, mislearn and misinform others [4].

This self-deception can be described as lying to ourselves to cope with life's frustrations. This happens when we are not mentally strong enough to be honest with ourselves. One common form of self-deception is the way we see our overweight condition. Often, we fail to accept that the rich food we are eating is the cause of our weight gain. We blame the scales or hope that a little run or exercise will take care of the extra weight. Self-deception in a leader can cause incalculable damage to the organization. Such a person looks at data selectively, has a favourable opinion of subordinates who follow his/her thinking and shuns others who don't agree. This leads to lack of trust and accountability. Communication breaks down. The result is poor decision-making. Richard Fuld, CEO of Lehman Brothers at the time of bankruptcy, always saw himself as a victim, never the perpetrator of this event.

Self-awareness provides us with greater control over our lives and the events which shape them. If we do not develop skills in self-awareness or we are in the mode of self-denial, we cannot gauge our strengths and weaknesses, our need and knowing what is retarding our growth, both personal and professional. Self-awareness is the first step in our journey of lifelong learning.

We need to list all the skills that we possess. It may include everything, things that you don't usually do for work. You may call me crazy when I list cooking as a professional skill. However, learning to cook taught me patience, precision, experimentation, etc. You may list down all of these skills. You will be astounded with the discovery of skills you never thought you possessed. Now discover which ones you could translate into money? However, you may not apply some of these skills for the sake of monetary benefits. Sometimes, you may just want to cook or sing with no desire for additional money. But out of the skills that you list that you would do for money, think of all the ways those skills can be used. We should start looking at ourselves as a collection of skills, competencies and knowledge which can be deployed in many circumstances. Generally, we see ourselves in the context of our present jobs and can overlook opportunities which are there or are opening up in future.

Preparing for the Future

The next step in preparing for the future is to do a stock-taking of what has been our experience in the past, whether our education has prepared us for the work we are doing today. One of the major complaints with higher education is that they tend to prepare students for jobs of the past.

Past learnings have a bearing on almost every action we take although for most of us learning remains an activity undertaken in, or associated with, formal education.

However, learning is a continuous process that commences at birth and continues until death; it is the process through which we use our experience to deal with new situations and to develop relationships.

What skills and competencies we have acquired in the recent past? What have been our failures? What has worked and what has not? Our past experiences are like building a wall. Each new event is built upon the experiences of the past. However, we do not consider our experiences as a sequence but unrelated events. Self-reflection is not always a happy recollection but is always rewarding. Sometimes we learn more from our failures than successes and we should develop the skills for regularly recalling our experiences and draw lessons from it. Our business schools teach us to look forward and we turn into leaders consumed with action. Only self-reflection prepares us to insight and complex learning and apply learning to novel problems or situations as they arise in future. We learn to discard what is obsolete or does not work and create mental space for new knowledge.

The perils of not reflecting are that we may continue to blame our environment for our lack of progress. The boss is partial, the company is not doing well, competition is tough, etc. Perhaps, we have not been bold enough to take up challenging and riskier assignment; perhaps, we are unwilling to leave the comfort and convenience at one city to move to a newer unknown destination.

What can be done to help in developing the critical, constructive and creative thinking, which is necessary for a reflective practice?

Neil Thompson, in his book *People Skills* [5], suggests that there are six steps:

1. Read around the topics you are learning about or want to learn about and develop
2. Ask others about the way they do things and why
3. Watch what is going on around you
4. Feel—pay attention to your emotions, what prompts them and how you deal with negative ones
5. Talk—share your views and experiences with others in your organization
6. Think—learn to value time spent thinking about your work

It's not just the thinking that's important! One has to develop an understanding and appreciation of others' too and then explore ideas with them. This reflective practice when done with trusted colleagues or family as a shared activity can increase manifold the benefits of reflection as a learning tool.

As an added exercise, it is advisable to start writing in a reflective learning diary as described further.

Quietly identify a situation you encountered at your work or in personal life that you believe could have been dealt with more effectively.

1. **Describe the experience**
   What happened? When and where did this situation occur? Are there any other thoughts you have on the situation?

2. Reflect

What was your behaviour? What kind of thoughts occurred to you? How did it make you feel? Were there any additional factors which influenced the situation? What were your learnings?

3. Theorize

How did the experience match with your preconceived ideas, that is, was the outcome expected or unexpected? What behaviour you think might have changed the outcome?

4. Experiment

Is there anything you could do or have done to change the outcome? What action(s) can you take to change similar reactions in the future? What behaviour might you attempt?

Read the entry after a month and with the advantage of hindsight, either on your own or in consultation with a trusted person, see if you have gained any additional insight into dealing with such situations in future and record it.

Learner or Growth Mindset

With self-awareness and reflection, one starts to develop a positive learner mindset. Have a positive mindset to accept that our knowledge will never be complete or whole and we have to keep learning continuously and expand our knowledge.

A mindset is a belief which determines how we see ourselves in our personality, talent and intelligence. We can view these as fixed traits which cannot be changed or these are things over which we have control to cultivate and change throughout our lives. Our mindsets control our limitations or potentials for growth. The roots to this understanding stem from the contributions by the Stanford Psychologist Carol Dweck, who researched on the power of our beliefs, both conscious and unconscious, and showed how by changing the simplest of them can have a long-term impact on every aspect of our lives. Mindset determines whether we are successful at what we do or join those who are always struggling.

According to Carol Dweck's research reported in her book *Mindset*, one of our fundamental beliefs is what we know about our personality. Those with fixed mindsets believe that intelligence or talent are fixed traits which cannot be changed in any meaningful way and our striving for success only reaffirms our inherent intelligence, and risky action which may lead to failure must be avoided as people would say that 'you failed in spite of such talent'.

Such people when they reach positions of authority stop taking bold decisions and deny hearing to those who bring innovative solutions. Leaders with fixed mindsets will surround themselves with people who agree with them, the 'yes men'. They look for friends or partners who will bolster their self-esteem. Their biggest fear is not to do anything which will make them look dumb. Such people lack resilience. They cannot believe that they can also fail and failure becomes a big setback, hence meaning either you are not smart or talented.

In contrast, a person with 'growth mindset' seeks and flourishes on challenging assignments. He views failure not as a deficiency of competency or skills but another step in the ladder for growth. Many successful people fail several times before achieving spectacular success. Abraham Lincoln was discharged from his command as captain, he failed as a businessman as well as a lawyer and failed in his first election for the legislature followed by Congress, Senate and later Vice-Presidency. Leaders with growth mindsets surround themselves with people who can challenge their thoughts and opinions. They are comfortable in the company of 'no men'.

People with 'growth mindset' believe that their skills, abilities and competencies can be changed through effort and IQ, and talent is only the starting point. They have a passion for learning and they develop resilience, which is the hallmark of all big achievements. All top achievers from Genghis Khan to Bill Gates had these qualities.

People with fixed mindset questions are reactive and automatic, leading to defensiveness, win–lose relating and a view of limited possibilities, while people with learner or growth mindset are flexible and adaptive, leading to questioning assumptions, win-win relating and a view of plentiful possibilities [6].

When Sheryl Sandberg, chief operating officer of Facebook, was asked: 'What's the number one thing you look for in someone who can scale with a company?'

Sandberg replied, 'Someone who takes feedback well. Because people who can take feedback well are people who can learn and grow quickly'. [7]

Carol Dweck further writes 'my research has shown that the view you adopt for yourself profoundly affects the way you lead your life. It can determine whether you become the person you want to be and whether you accomplish the things you value.'

People with growth mindset explore all opportunities to learn and grow. They learn from past experiences; they learn from mentors, peers and juniors; they learn from written and electronic media; and to be successful in a VUCA world, one cannot let go of any opportunity to grow.

Twenty years back, Steve Jobs gave an interview to the Silicon Valley Historical Association and gave some insight into what he believed to be the secret of a successful life.

> When you grow up, you tend to get told that the world is the way it is and your life is just to live your life inside the world, try not to bash into the walls too much. That's a very limited life. Life can be much broader once you discover one simple fact, and that is that everything around you that you call life was made up by people that were no smarter than you. You gotta act. And you gotta be willing to fail, you gotta be willing to crash and burn... if you're afraid of failing, you won't get very far. [8]

Not that everyone will become a leader. Sadly, most managers and even CEOs become bosses, not leaders. They wield power instead of transforming themselves, their workers and their organization.

Ursula Burns joined Xerox Corporation as a summer intern in 1980; she was named president in 2007, CEO in 2009 and Chairman in 2010. Burns became the first

African American woman to become CEO of a Fortune 500 company. She had neither an easy nor a direct path on her rise as chairman and CEO of Xerox.

> I didn't think, when I walked into the company, that I would be the CEO, I did expect to be successful, though. My mother raised us to think that if we worked hard, and if we put our end of the bargain in, it would work out OK for us. [9]
>
> It has been a fun looking back on my early years at the company with a reflection on the tremendous change. But, what hasn't changed, is the need to surround myself with a great, diverse team—people who can be trusted in providing me with a sound counsel, people who I can really listen to, and honest critics who I can rely on to tell it like it is—even when I may not want to hear it—and challenge me to be a better leader and a better person. I am still learning. [10]

Today, it has been evidenced that with the right attitude—that of a growth mindset—employees like Ursula Burns can learn and thrive.

Once you have set your mind to take the train to life-long learning, the first stop is know yourself and learn the knowledge and skills you possess by conducting a personal SWOT (strengths, weaknesses, opportunities and threats) analysis.

Conduct a Personal SWOT Analysis
One needs to introspect on how will one's job be different, a few years from now? Will the job or profile even exist in its present form, let's say in five years? And moreover

by that time, what will happen to the company and the industry employing you?

Technically speaking, we have no idea what the future holds for us. Yet what we do know for certain is that change will be constant at the workplace.

Can one predict and prepare for this unknown workplace of the future? Have you realized what should one be doing currently to make sure you don't find yourself facing an end in your career?

Do you review your CV at least once every six months, revising it to add achievements and skills added?

In the next stage of self-aware learning, a self-aware learner must know at any stage what are his/her current skills, knowledge and competency levels, what are the gaps he/she foresees which arise due to changing work needs and demands; and what actions the learner must undertake to minimize the gaps in his/her ability to retain present job and move to a more satisfactory level.

Conducting a personal SWOT analysis is the first step in that direction. One of the toughest things to achieve is to effectively carry out a skills self-evaluation while stating clear objectives in a personal learning plan (PLP).

A SWOT analysis is a strategy exercise generally used in business to assess a company, organization, group or problem area. It's a regimented brainstorming session that identifies the organization's strengths, weaknesses, opportunities and threats. This concept can be applied to personal growth too.

Personal SWOT analysis is a critical assessment of an individual's strengths, weaknesses, opportunities and threats. One must take an inward look at the following:

1. What can make a person valuable?
2. Which areas need to be honed on?
3. What things a person may take advantage of?
4. What threatens their ability to take advantage of opportunities?

At a given time, it is not an easy task in being objective with oneself. It depends on how we are as a person: a confident one with lower self-esteem will have diametrically opposed difficulties in evaluating both realistically and objectively.

A personal SWOT analysis can aid in gaining clarity while setting up realistic objectives. It is simple to use but can be further exploited with the help of a friend, family, coach or mentor. This person is someone that you trust and who trusts you and you accept what he/she has to say. It is someone whose opinion you value so that if they point out a weakness that you didn't think you had, you will listen and accept it as fact. It is someone from whom you can accept constructive criticism.

SWOT Matrix

The purpose of this exercise is to identify gaps in continuous learning and prepare a learning plan for oneself. One possible SWOT exercise which we have developed with scoring is given in the Annexure (Personal SWOT Analysis).

Some of the questions which a personal SWOT analysis attempts to answer are given after this paragraph (you can add more as you go along). This SWOT template was conceived by us when one of us was offered a VRS.

Strengths	Weaknesses
Strengths are the internal positive aspects that are in complete control (i.e., things you are really good at, value you have to offer, etc.). Some questions to ask are:	Weaknesses are the internal negative aspects that are under one's control but need improvement (i.e., lack of experience, limited knowledge, etc.). Some questions to ask are:
Experience: Are you currently a member of any cross-functional team?	Am I aware of my weaknesses? Do I have a list which I have analysed?
Have you in the past one year contributed to a cross-functional project as an ideator/team player/project leader?	What essential tasks do I typically do not enjoy and avoid?
Is the work you or your team does critical or core to the company's strategy or operations?	Have I invited feedback on my weaknesses from family members/friends/colleagues and subordinates in the past six months? Have they been forthcoming with their views or do they feel shy of telling me?
Have you been assigned any new work in the past six months?	
Have you been asked to do any special assignment not related to your job description in the past six months?	Have I taken active steps to overcome any weakness in past six months?
Have you made any suggestion which has been accepted or acted upon by your company in the past six months?	Should I lose my job today, do I have a contingency plan?
	What are obstacles to my growth—city/language/culture adjustment/relevant work experience family, age, etc.?

Has your boss asked for your opinion on any critical matter in the past three months?	What was your last increment compared to your peer group?
Networking: Are you a member of professional association/s?	
In any of your networks/associations, how many meetings have you attended in the past three months?	
How many possible new professional contacts have you got personally introduced to in the last meeting/conference you attended? I always make a point of meeting at least five new persons at any conference or meet and keep in touch by circulating relevant information, research and articles, etc.	
Are you an active member of social media? List some of your top contributions in the recent past.	
Are you currently mentoring a subordinate?	
Have you volunteered for any project at work or outside in the past six months?	

(continued)

(continued)

List some of the Big Risks you have taken in the last three years either for yourself, department or organization.	
Were you able to come up with appropriate risk management strategies to ensure that risks were not pure gambles?	
What do other members of your team/organization perceive as your strengths?	
Does top management/colleagues regularly involve you in their new initiatives?	
Which of your achievements are you most satisfied with? Have you analysed the key reasons?	
Developing Knowledge/Skills	
Have you read a book to develop fresh thoughts in a specific area in the past three months?	
Have you mapped your knowledge/skill/competency gaps in the past one year in comparison to what you feel is essential?	

Have you learnt any new skill in the past six months? Have you taken steps to reduce gaps with any specific steps (e.g., external programmes/reading/teaching/mentoring/any other)? Have you drawn a PLP? Have you checked out the resources that are available to you to help you close this gap?	
Opportunities	**Threats**
Opportunities are the positive external conditions that are not under one's control, but which can be taken advantage of (i.e., company growth, field shortage, etc.). Some questions to ask are: Do you have a systematic process to scan opportunities? Have you looked at opportunities in areas other than your current function in same company/same industry/different industry?	Threats are the negative external conditions that are not under one's control but the overall effect of which you may be able to dampen (i.e., field obsolescence, competition, etc.). Some questions to ask are: Do I have a list of possible threats to myself, my company and my industry? Have I started taking steps to help me counter these threats?

(continued)

(continued)

Have you recently brought any competitors' weaknesses/strengths to brainstorm with your team and colleagues? Has your opportunity scans led to significant new steps/initiatives in the last one year?	How effective are these steps in the overall analysis? Is your company performing well compared to its peers in the industry? How do the external analysts rate your company, the peer group and industry prospects over the next three years?

For example, your company or a competitor in its annual general meeting announced a new division to market new products. Do you have the knowledge or skills, or can you learn the new skills required in a short time to apply for this new opportunity? Presently, IT sector is undergoing a downturn but health care industry is expanding. You have no control over this, but by enhancing your transferable skills, you could more easily move into another industry.

Were you passed over for a promotion which you thought you deserved? After interviews, do you reflect on the questions you could not answer? Any clues to give an indication of any skills deficiency you may not have noticed till now?

Some threats cannot be avoided, but you can do things to make them less painful. You may not be able to do anything about a pending layoff, but you can make it less impactful by updating and floating your resume early, start networking in the industry, etc.

Always review your contingency plans as if your job is gone today. In addition, regularly study and analyse the changes happening at your workplace, especially internal re-organizations, new projects, new divisions, etc., the industry and the business environment. These combine both threats and opportunities. You may like to discuss these with your trusted peers and mentors in arriving at a personal growth strategy. This includes multi-skilling through seeking job rotation as Deepak (mentioned earlier) did, attending training programmes where you can use the skills learnt immediately at your work, attending conferences and seminars, where though I learnt very little but made valuable contacts for my network. Most of what I have learnt has been through leveraging my experience and continuously involved in informal learning.

Conducting a personal SWOT once is not enough. It must be repeated at least once every six months and scores compared with previous exercise to measure progress and identify areas still to be conquered.

Once you have gained insight into your skills gap, your train is ready to go to the next stop in its journey towards self-learning, that is, acquiring new knowledge and skills.

References

1. Kharpal, Arjun. 2017, 24 April. *Billionaire Jack Ma Says CEOs Could Be Robots in 30 Years, Warns of Decades of 'Pain' from A.I., Internet Impact.* Available at https://www.cnbc.com/2017/04/24/jack-ma-robots-ai-internet-decades-of-pain.html (accessed 8 February 2018).
2. Chideya, Farai. 2016. *The Episodic Career.* New York: Simon & Schuster. Johnson, Whitney. 2012, July–August.

'Disrupt Yourself'. *Harvard Business Review*. Available at https://hbr.org/archive-toc/BR1207?ab=Magazine%20 TOC-Links-Browse_Issues (accessed 16 April 2018).

3. Steiner, Patricia. 2014, 19 August. 'The Impact of the Self-awareness Process on Learning and Leading'. *The New England Journal of Higher Education*. Available at http://www.nebhe.org/thejournal/the-impact-of-the-self-awareness-process-on-learning-and-leading/ (accessed 8 February 2018).

4. https://repository.library.northeastern.edu/files/neu: cj82m223d/fulltext.pdf

5. Thompson, Neil. 2015. *People Skills*, 4th ed. London: Palgrave Macmillan.

6. Dweck, Carol. 2006. *Mindset; The New Psychology of Success*. New York: Penguin Random House.

7. Bariso, Justin. 2016, 31 October. *It Took Sheryl Sandberg Exactly 2 Sentences to Give the Best Career Advice You'll Hear Today*. Inc. Available at https://www.inc.com/justin-bariso/it-took-sheryl-sandberg-exactly-2-sentences-to-give-the-best-career-advice-youll.html (accessed 8 February 2018).

8. Dzombak, Dan. 2014, 30 September. *Steve Jobs' Secret of a Successful Life*. Available at http://www.dandzombak.com/steve-jobs-secret-of-life/ (accessed 22 May 2017).

9. Lean In. *Ursula M. Burns*. Available at https://leanin.org/stories/ursula-burns/ (accessed 22 May 2017).

10. Burns, Ursula. 2015, 25 September. *After 35 Years at Xerox, Ursula Burns is Still Learning*. Fortune. Available at http://fortune.com/2015/09/25/xerox-ceo-ursula-burns-leadership-lesson/ (accessed 8 February 2018).

Chapter 5
I Am My Own Teacher

The wisest mind has something yet to learn.

—George Santayana

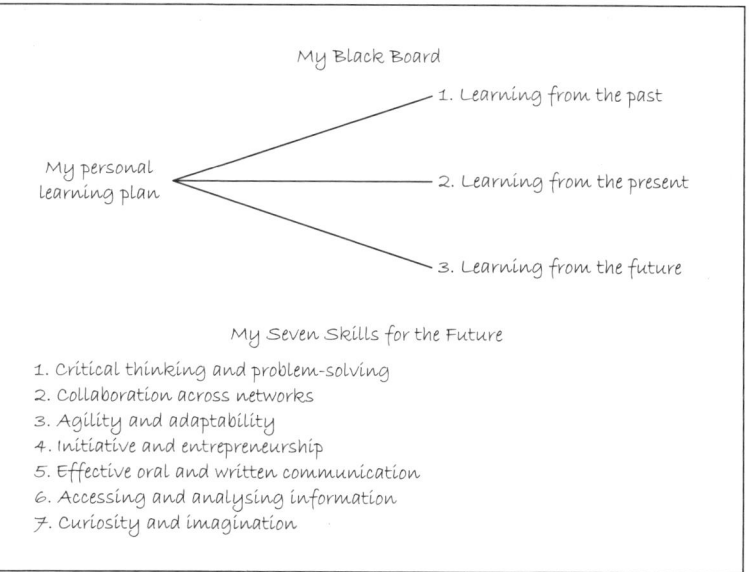

Today's learners and workplace learning environment are vastly different than they were even 10 years back. Learning is often confused with training. The first question to ponder is what is learning? Learning is a change in behaviour, while in training, an individual seeks a change in knowledge or skill. Training can be a source of learning if the learner has an opportunity or aptitude to apply the lessons learnt in the workplace. The very reason that in spite of spending millions of dollars in staff training, minimal change is apparent because maybe there is little change in the workplace environment. For example, companies send thousands of managers each year on training for teamwork but do not create an effective environment for teamwork. The appraisal is still based on an individual's performance. Therefore, there is little change in behaviour. In a company I (Abidi) worked for, there was a large field force and every year the company's ranking in customer perception remained between 10 and 12 in industry rankings in spite of having one of the largest training department in the industry. So what went wrong? Was it assessment of individuals or the assessment of a system as a whole?

Adults learn differently from children. Unlike children, they accumulate experience throughout their life. Adult behaviour is not only influenced by learning, it also influences learning by sharing knowledge. Therefore, it is interesting to know how adults differ from that of children in the learning process:

Adults

1. have the need to know why they are learning something

2. have a need to be self-directed
3. bring more work-related experience into the learning situation
4. enter into a learning experience with a problem-centred approach to learning
5. are motivated to learn by both extrinsic and intrinsic motivators [1]

Today's dynamic and complex work environments may provide ample opportunities for learning, but in the haste of action the potential for informal learning may be overlooked. Informal learning is the learning that takes place outside the formal boundaries of classroom as in corporate training and development. The combined learning from a heterogeneous group is the key differentiator. Adults often feel like they just can't learn things as quickly as when you were a child. It seems like whereas information used to be soaked up like a sponge, it takes a lot longer to learn new things later in life. Are adults just not as good at learning as children, or do they learn in a different way? Adults and children are not necessarily better or worse learners than each other, they just learn differently. Is it the ability to learn or willingness to learn in question? Or that the relative ability towards learning and willingness to learn recedes as the age goes up?

Adults are self-directed learners, whereas younger students are dependent on adults. The traditional learning model naturally requires that children depend upon adults for the next lesson, the next assignment and the next subject matter. Adult learning turns this paradigm on its head by making the study of most subjects a self-directed endeavour.

Adults challenge new information due to their accumulated memory. New information is not accepted unless its conflict with existing embedded information is resolved. However, young students implicitly accept it. For adults, scepticism and hesitation to accept new knowledge is a natural path to learning and must be encouraged. The following progression shows that adults learn by challenging new ideas, comparing them to their existing mindsets, life lessons and other information, thereby reinforcing the new information, concepts and ideas into their minds. Adults frequently also discard old knowledge to make way for the new.

Curiosity → investigation → discovery → challenge → action → reflection → change

The objective of adult learning is immediate use and relevance, while students engage in education to build a foundation for use later in life. An adult learns through dialogue, while the student is a passive recipient of information. Adults accept responsibility for their own learning, whereas responsibility of young students' education is shouldered by adults such as parents, guardians or teachers. Adult learning never ends. It is a continuous process and very dynamic by nature. It changes with environment and needs. Adults are able to bring all of their life experiences to the situation, which will add to their learning and help them to understand new information. Learning should be seen as a living, breathing organism. It must be permitted to expand, to grow and to develop. It is not a static thing. It cannot be set in stone. As the world changes, so must the adult. This is what we say preparing for the future.

Therefore, by definition, adult learning is the entire range of formal, non-formal and informal learning activities which are undertaken by adults which results in the acquisition of new knowledge and skills.

This is how adults should be learning in theory, but in practice things do not turn out to be so neat. Adults are not as good as infants in pursuit of curiosity. The influence of parents (do this or not do that) or their staid expectations, teacher's rote style of imparting knowledge and finally the line and staff organization of the corporate environment where conformity is valued and frequent questioning is frowned upon puts a stop to curiosity.

According to Albert Einstein, curiosity has its own reason for existence and the most important thing is that students should not stop questioning. The art of questioning and curiosity to learn are basics, impregnated into the genes of a human being, yet a few really use it wisely. The assembly line rote system of learning practised in India was introduced by the British rulers and was designed to produce an army of clerks, that is, producing non-curious students. University of California (UC) recently conducted series of experiments to understand what exactly goes on in the brain when our curiosity is aroused. Their three most important research findings were that curiosity prepares brain for learning, curiosity makes subsequent learning more rewarding and curiosity makes learning more effective and enjoyable [2].

All growth lies in the territory of the unknown. What we already know is in the past. What we have yet to discover is the future. There has to be a connection between them as well as the correct alignment. An organization which promotes curiosity by encouraging employees to ask questions and rock the status quo will continue drawing the organization and its employees into a bigger future with new possibilities. The challenge is how to harness intensive learning through the art of questioning!

Experience alone is no guarantee of lifetime growth. By questioning the status quo, you can continually transform the experiences into newer lessons and one can make each day of life a source of growth.

At the workplace, leaders make bigger mistakes as they refuse to accept that even with higher intelligence, they can also commit mistakes and continue to blame others. I (Abidi) worked in the technical services department of a large company. The department's task was to help production in solving problems. A new technology for wastewater treatment was introduced and my boss decided to install it in the company's plant. The experimental technology never worked well but the boss did not accept the inevitable. He continued to blame his subordinates for its poor performance. The subordinates began to fudge records to show that the technology is working as expected. The whole charade ended when the boss was transferred on a promotion and his successor ditched the technology.

In addition, the memory of adults also comes in the way of new learning. Without reflection, people are unable to discard old knowledge to make way for the new. A bad experience derails our ability to seek the new. Over a lifetime, one collects obstacles in the shape of unverified assumptions and fixed mindsets, a sort of fortress around us, which come in the way of lifetime learning. A toddler falls at least a thousand times before learning to walk, while we give after one or two attempts. We have to rekindle our inner child to unleash the potential we possess.

The Indian cricket team won World Cup in 2011 under the captaincy of Mahendra Singh Dhoni but only four months later in April 2011, Dhoni and his men bit the dust magnificently in the test match series against England, losing 4–0, including two inning defeats. Resilient leaders understand that sustainable aspects of a long career will include both failures and successes, either coming first or following each other. The resilient leader looks at his failures as learning opportunities, a strategy to rise again. Dhoni bounced back and in 2013 broke Saurav Ganguly's record of most wins by an Indian captain in tests.

As against Dhoni, 48-year-old Phaneesh Murthy, popularly known as the 'other Murthy' at Infosys, had a meteoric career at India's second largest IT services firm. He donned many roles and was credited with taking the Infosys brand global as the company's global sales head along with company founders N. R. Narayana Murthy and Nandan Nilekani. They took Infosys' US revenues from $2 million to over $700 million under his stewardship as global sales head. The company had begun to actively groom him and promote him publicly, making him a director of Infosys and Infosys BPO in 2000.

And he threw it all away by getting into an ill-judged relationship and was charged with sexual harassment. Infosys was quick to give him the boot.

Yet Phaneesh was able to resurrect his career and image by founding Quintant Services with the backing of GMR

Group. It took over California-headquartered iGate. Murthy was given the task of turning iGate into a globally competitive and profitable IT services company. After eight years at iGate, serving as the company's president and CEO from 2008, Murthy's business acumen and leadership abilities were backed by private equity major Apax Partners when he made a bold bid to buy Mumbai-based IT company Patni Systems for $1.22 billion. Patni was double the size of iGate. It was a leveraged acquisition, the biggest in Indian IT, betting on Murthy's prowess to pull faster growth in a slowing outsourcing industry. The Patni deal made Murthy the chief of a billion-dollar enterprise [3].

However, Phaneesh did not learn from his first failure and was again fired from iGate for a similar and repeated misconduct with an employee. Murthy admitted regretting repeating the gross mistakes.

When leaders fail after a spectacular success, are there any strategies and approaches for a turnaround? Unfortunately, for both businesses and sport, the lessons lie more in failures than in success. Failure offers more opportunities to learn than success. As leadership expert and ex-director of IIM Kozhikode Debashis Chatterjee says: "'For an evolving leader failure is feedback". Failure, unlike success comes with double loop learning: (a) What were the elements of failure (b) What needs to be done from here in order to succeed. Success only helps you learn from a single loop (b)' [4].

Dhoni learnt from his mistakes and moved forward. Phaneesh did not and suffered repeated setbacks. Learning from failures is just one of the learnings one can engage in over a lifetime, and a learning leader takes his/her growth like climbing a mountain. Sometimes there would be sharp ascents, followed by descent and plateau. His/her accumulated learning ultimately takes him/her to the top.

Our organizational culture also comes in the way of acquiring new knowledge. Our line and staff structure prevents across-the-board interactions and networking. Little emphasis and sometimes little understanding of the role of informal learning in creating new knowledge, fear of experimentation and failure are some of the factors which prevent individuals from acquiring and applying new knowledge to solve organizational problems.

For example, salespersons in showrooms of vehicles too gather valuable insights into customer behaviour and competitive landscape as they are continuously learning and accumulating new knowledge from their interactions with customers. However, they are rarely consulted on strategic matters.

Once you have embarked on the journey of lifetime learning, where do you begin from? We start by creating our PLP. It consists of:

1. Learning from the Past
   Leveraging our own experience, both successful and, especially, failure. Failure may not be catastrophic but failure to learn would certainly be.

2. Learning from the Present
   One must conduct a personal SWOT analysis at least once every six months. Identify gaps in competencies and skills and take necessary steps to upgrade. Create

or join one or more learning or professional groups on the Internet like LinkedIn, etc.

3. Learning from the Future
   Future does not come imminently; it only seems so because we have been unable to see the early signs or cues. Cultivating a regular reading habit as lifelong learning, networking and meeting new people would make one in taking newer challenges before others get to see it.

Learning from the Past

Every night before sleeping, I (Abidi) reflect on the day's events and derive insights into my events of the day, especially my behaviour, and seek changes. What did I do new today; what did I do wrong? What did I do right? What questions could I not answer? Did I waste a large amount of time on Facebook and so on? Did I acquire new knowledge and challenges in my profession? Whom did I learn from and what? etc.

Continuous learning is an essential journey for a lifetime growth. One can have a variety of experiences but still remain as before. Experience itself is not a definite guarantee of lifetime growth. But if you regularly transform your experiences into newer lessons, each day will be a perfect source of learning followed by high growth. Smart people are those who can transform even the smallest incidents into sources of extraordinary learning. Emperor Babur wrote in his autobiography *Baburnama* that early in his life, he had an obsession with the conquest of the rich kingdom of Samarkand. He was defeated, lost his small kingdom and was driven to lead a life of a nomad in deep mountains with few supporters. One day, he heard a commotion outside his tent and enquired what had happened. A soldier told him that a wolf had been coming for past three days to hunt for a meal. The first day, it went into the horses' enclosure but was kicked out and had to retreat swiftly. The next day, the wolf entered the sheep's enclosure and when the sheep started baying loudly, it retreated again. However, last night, when the wolf entered the chicken coop, it got away with one chicken. Babur reflected that the wolf was smarter than he was. It was not obsessed with one objective and with each failure, the wolf would proceed to another one till it succeeded. On the contrary, he (Babur) remained obsessed with Samarkand. This narration and observation led to a fast learning and hence, Babur then decided to look elsewhere to fulfil his destiny. He started thinking about India.

Failure will continue to thwart your efforts. Resilience and adaptability are skills that should be in every person's learning toolkit. These skills shall come through developing and regularly using of the power of reflection. This implies revisiting on personal experiences and identifying what went wrong and how to rectify it. Now you are on the road to be a self-directed learner.

Learning from the Present

Every day when you get up, ask yourself a question 'What will happen if I lose my job today?' Do you have a contingency plan? Regularly review your contingency plans as if your job is lost today. In addition, do regularly study on changes taking place around and in your company, especially internal reorganizations, new projects, new divisions, etc., the industry and the business environment in general. All of these present threats and opportunities. Regularly discuss these with your trusted peers and mentors, and craft your personal growth strategy. This must include multi-skilling via job rotation, participating in training programmes, attending conferences and seminars where new skills can be learnt and tested immediately, besides making valuable contacts for your network. Most of what I have learnt has been through leveraging my personal experience and getting involved in informal learning continuously [5]. Every morning, before getting out of the bed, promise to yourself that you will definitely do something new today. One must unlearn the past and create space for new knowledge which will aid in sharpening the skills.

Intelligence gathering is focused on the present and relies on developing skills in uncovering and using available data and information relevant today. Over 70 per cent of information in databases is unutilized due to lack of information-handling skills. Employees who are aware of their business environment and possess analytical skills to interpret this can provide innovative solutions and road maps for their organization's growth.

Learning from the Future

Going boldly where no one has gone before is key to survival and career progress in a VUCA world. How will your career be different a few years from now? Will your job even exist? In 5 to 10 years, will even your company or industry exist? Individuals as well as firms and industry must seek challenges to fight its own inertia. The rules for tomorrow shall change rapidly and so will be the turbulence generated as a result. There will be a vortex around. Only the smart learners will scale up, rest shall remain in low-paying jobs. Have you started seeing this vortex around you?

We know one thing about future. It is that change is the only reality, which can be foreseen. We also know that what we will do in future will be different from what we are doing today. How can we prepare for the future which we cannot even see clearly to ensure that we, when time comes for a change, are not left sitting on a bench, waiting for a train which has changed its platform? Keep your career paths open in all directions where, even if your job description may not be relevant in the future, your skills can still be used or you can acquire new competencies and skills for new careers coming up the horizon. We are entering an era of episodic careers where each career is an episode and your past experience may not be relevant for future careers.

The first step in learning is the realization that change is constant. You can then take control of your future career through foresight and planning. You can develop a mental radar which is always scanning the horizon and alerting you to early indications of change and thus prepare you to capitalize on emerging opportunities.

Therefore, our continuous learning must be built on a foundation for acquiring essential or survival skills which are critical for whatever the future brings, which will allow us to quickly move to whichever direction our career takes us. It should ensure that we can make directional changes in our career without crashing out. They will help you keep your skills up to date and your opportunities wide open.

Learning from past, present and future must be embedded through seven survival skills for the future. These skills are not taught but can be learnt.

Seven Survival Skills for the Future

The objective of our education system, especially management education, is to impart technical skills but, as we are witnessing in the real world, the need is to enhance soft skills, which are not taught in the business schools and are outside the realm of textbooks. Scoring grades in examinations are considered the most important outcome of education, but in today's world, this alone cannot promise a satisfactory career. At best, it can give you a jump-start. Therefore, companies put in a lot of effort to train fresh MBAs before the employees can be expected to show results. As said earlier, these graduates pass out from a 'celebrated rote system' and not the 'school of learning' where curiosity and questioning are embraced. Tony Wagner, fellow at the Harvard University states that

> Today knowledge is ubiquitous, constantly changing, growing exponentially.... Today knowledge is free. It's like air, it's like water. It's become a commodity.... There's no competitive advantage today in knowing more than the person next to you. The world doesn't care what you know. What the world cares about is what you can do with what you know. [6]

The work culture of the 21st century demands multiple areas of competency within an individual. The competencies and skills once acquired may not last a lifetime. These become obsolete and one has to learn new skills. Careers themselves are becoming a series of episodes, with the new one having little relationship with the past one. Therefore, one needs to master survival skills which become an anchor for whatever the future has in store, a set of super skills, which can be applied in all circumstances.

In teaching 21st-century skills, Tony Wagner, an educator and innovator, introduced seven survival skills [7] which should be in everyone's portfolio, whether you are a student getting ready for your first job, new executive, middle level, senior level or a professional and even self-employed.

These skills are more important than academic knowledge. These skills are not taught but can be learnt. These are:

1. Critical thinking and problem-solving
   As the world economy shifts away from creating jobs in manufacturing and towards service industry for new jobs, there's a consensus among business leaders that it is crucial that students graduating from universities or the workforce equip themselves with the ability to identify and solve complex problems, think critically about information, work effectively in teams and communicate clearly about their thinking.

   Critical thinking is being consistently rated by most employers as being a set of skill that is increasing its importance. The study reflected that over 49 per cent of employers quantified their employees' critical thinking skills as only or below average. In fact, only 28 per cent of employers rated four-year graduates as having 'excellent' critical thinking skills [8]. The US Department of Labor has identified that critical thinking is a new raw material for number of key workplace skills, such as problem-solving, decision-making, organizational planning and risk management [9]. Critical thinkers are accomplished at logical reasoning, use facts and believe that there can be more than one road map to the desired outcome and they can leverage this adaptable approach for reaching optimal results. Companies value critical thinkers for what they bring to the table, namely, the ability to challenge the status quo.

The idea that a company's senior leaders have all the answers and can solve problems by themselves is no longer true. In fact, the workers who are close to customers such as automobile showroom salespersons, people who work at the intersection of two disciplines such as marketing and R&D may have more insights about customers, products, features, complaints, early warnings, etc., than people who make decisions. However, to convert ideas and insights into practical implementable solutions require all employees to develop critical thinking and collaborative skills; collaborative because today no one, including the most qualified expert, has total knowledge but with collaboration and information sharing, complete knowledge can be gained.

A study done in 1989 by Sidney Yoshida called *The Iceberg of Ignorance* [10] suggested that senior level management is often so far removed from day-to-day business operations that they fail to understand the systems and processes that affect both employees and customers. The most alarming result of this study suggests that this iceberg of ignorance can have an impact on company profits by as much as 40 per cent. Most organizations of all kinds have the knowledge embedded in their employees which can be harnessed by a humble leader who is willing to listen and learn.

Critical thinking consists of three essential parts: recognizing assumptions, weighing evidence and drawing conclusions. This may be termed as receptive–adaptive–interpretative mechanism towards critical thinking.

Recognizing assumptions is the ability to separate fact from opinion. The next is weighing evidence. How do we know what's true and false? What is the evidence, and is it credible? Next, we should be aware of varying viewpoints. What viewpoint are we hearing? Who is the author, and what are his/her intentions? How might it look to someone with a different history? Develop insights into finding connections, and cause and effect. Is there a pattern? How are things connected? Where have we seen this before?

We come to conclusion by speculating on possibilities and conjectures. What if? Supposing that? Can we imagine alternatives?

Usually, we chase arguments which reinforce our beliefs and discard those which challenge it. This is more common with senior leaders such as CEOs. The successful CEOs are those who welcome arguments which challenge their own.

In a group where I worked, one company's financials were on a downward spiral and a team was sent to its plant to reduce costs. One of the biggest costs was fuel used in the furnace which used expensive LPG as fuel, as recommended by the Japanese collaborators, 20 years back. When a suggestion was made to replace LPG by fuel oil which was one-sixth the cost, the management shot down the proposal with the argument that fuel oil would deposit sulphur on the product reducing its magnetic property. This was a sheer assumption and there was no scientific basis for it. The real reason was an aversion to change and risk-taking. When a consultant carried out an experiment, it was found that small deposits of sulphur had no effect on the properties of product passing through the furnace. Later, this was also corroborated by the Japanese collaborators. Thus, the fuel was changed which saved a significant amount for the company and helped made the product competitive in the market.

Those who master this skill can bring information from disparate sources together to come to a conclusion that is logical, following the evidence or facts available. They refrain from generalizing beyond facts and readily change their stand when facts warrant doing so. Such people are said to have 'good judgement' as they typically arrive at a quality decision. In general, when information is presented to them, people alternate between accepting assumptions and evaluating evidence. Critical thinkers, on the other hand, recognize the presence of both faulty assumptions and weak evidence, which improves the likelihood of arriving at an optimal decision. With concentrated practice over time, typically several months, critical thinking skills can be significantly honed.

Critical thinking, perhaps more than any other business skill set, can make the difference between success and failure. Fortunately, these skills are not out of reach—they are readily available to employees at all levels. Once gained, critical thinking skills last a lifetime and become a powerful asset for organizations seeking a competitive edge [11].

Let us examine the case of critical thinking in practice. In India, we are looking at the debt trap of many companies of which Essar Group is a symptomatic example. The Group, now led by second-generation promoters, has a combined debt of around $20 billion. Very recently, Prashant Ruia, one of the promoters of Essar Group, at the time of sale of its Essar Oil assets to a Russian consortium, said that 'Could've been conservative, but in 2008–2009 everyone was chasing growth' [12]. Another company of the Group facing bankruptcy is Essar Steel. Why these assets came up for sale is a study in lack of critical thinking in organizations. When the sole aim is to become 'big', chasing Tata, Birla and other big business houses, many companies, where decision-making is limited to a few, especially a cabal of family members who tend to think alike, suffer from a deficiency in critical thinking as an organizational asset. Chasing targets on borrowed money without pausing to learn and build is a sure recipe for failure. Unlike Tata, where there is a considerable empowerment within company management, many family-run firms rely on a few trusted individuals for decision-making. Essar Group refused to learn any lessons from an earlier failure when in 1999 Essar Steel defaulted on floating rate notes worth $250 million issued to foreign investors.

The Economist noted that 'Conglomerates sometimes sell their least promising units, thereby ginning up returns for the remaining empire. But groups saddled with huge debts do not have that luxury; only by disposing of the most profitable parts can they raise enough funds to satisfy creditors'. By the time Ruia concludes the sale of its crown jewels, the Essar Group will shrink to a third of its peak revenues of $27 billion in 2014–2015. 'We look forward to being more prudent', says Prashant Ruia [13].

The Group went on buying diverse companies around the world including a BPO firm during a period of downturn with pressure on commodities business such as oil and steel, their principal businesses. Two of their steel acquisitions in Canada and the United States have filed for bankruptcy. Their power projects too have the sword hanging over their head.

This is a textbook case of decision-making based on untested assumptions. From 2006, they went on an expansion spree and invested $18 billion from 2011 to 2017. The thinking process of Essar Group promoters is a typical trap for failure where it is assumed that future is predictable and controllable, and you can leverage high debt to create resources which will pay off the debts. The truth is that in a VUCA world, future is unpredictable and cautious, and measured action is required. This debt trap issue has been played out in numerous companies and a detailed argument is given in our book *The VUCA Company*. The basic cause was the speed at which the second-generation promoters wanted to move up, throwing caution, which comes from deep thinking, to the wind.

Sunil Mittal, chairman of telecom company Bharti Airtel, recently said:

> We all must have made lots of mistakes. Lots of decision when you look back, say I wish they were better thought through. If you pin me down to one, I would say in 2010 our decision to go to Africa was a bit rushed and that has taken 6-7-8 years and lot of resources and my personal time to fix that. [14]

We will discuss more of learning in family firms in Chapter 8.

2. Collaboration across networks
    New knowledge is created at the intersection of two or more disciplines, for example, R&D and marketing, and marketing and sales. Ability to collaborate across lines and staff within the company and across other stake-holders such as vendors and government is an essential

skill for moving to senior positions. Collaboration leads to viewing problems from different perspectives, leading to uncovering new knowledge and finally delivering innovation.

In a case of collaboration between different units of a company manufacturing high precision, small dimension dental implants led to a new business of manufacturing auto parts with the same high precision technology. When their automotive clients saw their ultraclean sterilized rooms where the delicate dental implants are produced, they realized that they can order more sophisticated and precise automotive parts from this company.

Everybody knows that children's backpack is getting heavier by the year. Besides books and stationery, they carry laptops, food and drinks, and other items to facilitate learning. Collaboration between a children's hospital and a stationery company led them to co-design a backpack with compartments that balance the weight, avoid the movement of the content in the backpack and fasten to the child's chest with ergonomic and safety straps.

Working in companies which believe in active collaboration and as well as participating in project teams which work across disciplines can not only hone your ability to learn from others but also bring you to the notice of prospective employers as well as alert you to changing career opportunities within and outside the present work environment.

3. Agility and adaptability
   When Jack Welch announced his successor in 2001, the surprise was total. Jeff Immelt was everything Jack Welch was not. Jack Welch was a command and control type of leader, while low-key, humble Immelt was a consensus builder. Jack Welch said after the announcement that

   > [H]e (Immelt) apparently demonstrated a superior capacity to grow, which was the most important criterion in the choice. Welch and the directors knew they could never envision the challenges a CEO might face 15 years into the job. They just knew he would have to rethink and reinvent GE. Immelt demonstrated, in Frank Rhodes' phrase, the 'most expansive thinking'. [15]

   Even Jack Welch knew that days for his type of leadership were over. As Jeff Immelt remarked, 'I am a different generation from Jack … I have a different view of the world'.

   Clay Parker, former CEO at BOC Edwards and an engineer by training, remarked that anyone who works for him 'has to think, be flexible, change and be adaptive, and use a variety of tools to solve new problems'. He added: 'I can guarantee the job I hire someone to do will change or may not exist in the future, so this is why adaptability and learning skills are more important than technical skills' [16]. On the contrary, we do hear a lot on how leaders with bad intentions, as a result of fear of their existence, destroy those more knowledgeable and competent around them.

What organizations need to take into account is the need to be adaptable and to increase the focus on agility, so as to be able to execute change better and get new products and services to market faster. To keep pace, businesses need to embrace the value of adaptability. In a world in which one picture, one thought, one tweet can go viral in a few minutes, the only certainty is that there is no permanence.

In 2013, Nike's CEO Mark Parker, considered by many as the world's most creative CEO, said, 'One of my fears is being this big, slow, constipated, bureaucratic company that's happy with its success', adding, 'Companies fall apart when their model is so successful that it stifles thinking that challenges it' [17].

Zara is the brightest star of the fast-changing fashion industry. Zara's strategy involves adapting couture designs, manufacturing items and distributing products to stores mere two to three weeks after they first appear on Catwalk. In addition, store managers and sales teams continuously monitor trends and customer preferences and report them to designers at headquarters. Zara's key operational theme is one of agility. Its product development, manufacturing and supply chain processes— some of which are a radical departure from the normal practices in fast fashion—are expressly designed and implemented for agility.

When *Harvard Business Review* looked at Zara in 2004, it called Zara's management practices 'questionable, if not downright crazy'. The company can design, produce and deliver a new garment and put it on display in its stores worldwide in a mere 15 days. Such a pace is unheard-of in the fashion business, where designers typically spend months planning for the next season.' Dr Warren H. Hausman, professor of management science and engineering at Stanford University, has quantified the financial value of fast fashion to reduce unwanted markdowns and lost sales, or stock-outs, enabling firms to increase profits by as much as 28 per cent. Zara, says Hausman, achieves four times more profitability than most apparel retailers, by combining higher turn and margins, and lower inventory risk in a highly uncertain business [18].

Agility, resilience and adaptability are the three most import skills any person must acquire, whatever their level and area of work. We should be able to quickly see career opportunities appearing on the horizon, both within the company and outside it and ensure that skills and competencies are acquired to capture these moments. This is especially true in future when we see episodic careers appearing which have little co-relation to your past training or experience.

4. Initiative and entrepreneurship
    It is assumed that the definition of entrepreneurship is limited to starting a new business and venturing out on your own. However, in the evolving corporate world of empowered employees, entrepreneurship takes a totally different meaning. If the meaning can be changed to a person who spots opportunities and takes risk to achieve his/her goals, as an employee it could be

leading or joining a new path-breaking division, taking initiative to suggest strategic and operational ideas to raise the top or bottom line and then gathering a peer group to fine-tune the idea and present an innovation too (which are the traits of an internal entrepreneur). The balance seven skills listed here such as critical thinking, networking, effective communication, etc., can help a person rise within the organization through initiative and entrepreneurship.

Even in starting and sustaining a new business, the very reason that makes start-ups a graveyard of new initiatives reflects that possessing a narrow skill set of technology is not enough. According to a study, most start-ups fail because of four major reasons, that is, business model not being viable (poor strategic depth), running out of cash (poor knowledge of finance especially working capital), not enough interaction (little focus on users or customers) and lack of financing/investors (investors seeing failure ahead of the entrepreneur). The sum total is narrow skill set, especially critical, to jump from being an innovator to a businessperson.

The very thought of risk-taking tells us that we may not always be successful and sometimes failure is inevitable. Therefore, resilience is a foremost behaviour trait of a successful entrepreneur.

5. Effective oral and written communication
English is now the world language for business and many companies expect their executives to be conversant in this language. However, 'The National Employability

Report (Engineers)' issued by Aspiring Minds shows that among engineers, in India, only 2.9 per cent candidates have spoken English skills for high-end jobs in corporate sales/business consulting. Our training assignments also show the woeful lack of English language skills among participants [19].

My (Abidi) own experience in international trade has revealed that hundreds of exporters with rudimentary communication skills attend international trade shows with little to show for their efforts. Even for English language, they hire translators. Without language skills, you cannot read, converse, collaborate and even search Google effectively. There are forecasters who claim that the English language shall attain the status of the world language in the next 50 years. In China, over 20 million people are learning English language.

Business is expanding beyond borders, and companies are collaborating with its geographically diversified units and collaborators through video conferencing and other distance communication tools. The people working at these companies must have an excellent grasp of the English language.

6. Accessing and analysing information
   In the Introduction, we quoted from the book *Five Minds for the Future*, by Harvard educational psychologist Professor Howard Gardner, the need for developing the synthesizing mind, the ability to make sense of disparate information to seek connections, the ability to develop skill to take information from different

sources, the ability to understand and evaluate that information objectively and put it together in ways that make sense to the synthesizer and also to other persons.

Whatever we do, whether conversing on mobile, shopping or travelling, we leave a trail of data. Billions of bytes of data every day. 'Data is the new oil', a resource which is useless in its raw form but valuable when it is converted into insights. IoT will further accelerate this process. Companies have already started reaping benefits of converting data into knowledge, and people who are adept at that will be the most valuable assets. They would help companies understand their customers better and offer products and services tailored to their customers' needs.

To give an example, a recent job summary for a senior manager, customer insights and analytics (a post which did not exist a few years back), identifies finding insights from the huge amount of information, a key skill for this position, and make recommendations and provide strategic input based on quantifiable data from multiple sources.

The market for data analysts alone will grow from 10 per cent of IT professionals today to over one-third in a few years, and there is a huge deficit on the supply side. Analytics will become a key competitive factor in decision-making in strategy, risk management, financial performance and better customer relationship, among others. A study of McKinsey Global Institute states that the United States will face a shortage of about

190,000 data scientists and 1.5 million managers and analysts who can understand and make decisions using big data by 2018. The talent scarcity is most for data scientists, who can perform analytics, and analytics consultant, who can provide insights from this data. There are hundreds of related job titles which will see sharp growth such as data statistician, business intelligence developer, data architect, etc. India can reap this dividend as such work gets increasingly outsourced.

7. Curiosity and imagination
   What if? Can there be another way? Can it be done better? These are the questions which are asked and also answered by people skilled in curiosity and imagination. These are the people who would be solving tough problems and would be most valuable employees to retain sustainable jobs. All jobs which are routine will be automated.

   Curiosity and imagination is the beginning of the process of innovation. In fact, no civilization was possible without someone asking what if. Start asking yourself these questions. Observe keenly around you. You will find ideas for new markets and innovative products and services. Be receptive to what your mind is telling you. There is an insatiable thirst in the world for a regular stream of novel ideas and innovative products.

   Mughal Emperor Babur had an inquisitive mind and took great notice of the world around him. As ruler of Kabul, he would talk to caravan masters passing through his kingdom. They were the search engines, the Google, of that age, who were familiar with developments beyond the borders. From one such conversation, Babur learnt that the Ottomans had given a crushing defeat to the Persians through the use of a new type of 'bow' which emitted smoke instead of an arrow. His curiosity was aroused, and he immediately sent a general to the Ottoman Sultan to learn about this new 'bow'. The deployment of gunpowder made his victory possible at the first battle of Panipat which laid the foundation of Mughal Empire. The loser, Delhi's Sultan Sikandar Lodhi, had also heard of gunpowder but showed no curiosity in pursuing it further.

J. K. Rowling, the bestselling author of Harry Potter books, came from a family where her imagination was seen as

> [A]n amusing personal quirk that would never pay a mortgage, or secure a pension.... We do not need magic to change the world, we carry all the power we need inside ourselves already: we have the power to imagine better.... Many prefer not to exercise their imaginations at all. They choose to remain comfortably within the bounds of their own experience, never troubling to wonder how it would feel to have been born other than they are. [20]

Jobs and careers which require inquisitiveness, curiosity and imagination, that is, the deployment of critical thinking, are safe from outsourcing, replacement by automation or robots. Therefore, keep a childlike curiosity alive through questioning and exploring, which generate new theories, approaches, perspectives, dilemmas and ultimately learning to solve problems.

As your first or early job, look for an 'academy' company rather than the one which pays most, of which the leading examples are GE, Toyota, Amazon, Google and Genpact in India. Working here enables you to acquire the seven survival skills. Look for companies where leaders create and support an environment for imagination and creativity. The culture in such companies values individuality and ideas coming from even the most junior person. These companies encourage risk-taking and are not put off by failures.

Thomas J. Watson Jr., CEO of IBM from 1957–1971 created such an 'academy' company. According to one anecdote, Tom Watson called a vice president to his office to discuss a failed development project that lost IBM in the range of $10 million. Expecting to be fired, the vice president presented his letter of resignation. Tom Watson Jr. just shook his head: 'You are certainly not leaving after we just gave you a $10 million education' [21].

We have a great desire for learning, it is in our DNA since the days our ancestors lived in caves but somehow gets extinguished as we grow up. We all know the story of Nobel Prize winner Pakistan's Yousafzai Malala who was shot by religious bigots and nearly died. Sultana is an Afghan girl from the same mould. She lives in Taliban territory and when she was in fifth grade, her father received a warning that if Sultana persists in going to school, she will be disfigured. Since that time, she has been educating herself at home. She taught herself English from old newspapers and magazines and a Pashto-English dictionary. When the Internet was installed in her house, her self-learning took flight. She took lessons from Khan Academy (see Chapter 6) in mathematics. She continues to take lesson from Coursera (see Chapter 6). Her admirers in the United States got her admission in a college but the US government refused her a visa [22]. A loss for the United States and the world.

A VUCA world needs people who are self-directed learners, whose learning does not stop after obtaining a degree or diploma. They are skilled in obtaining the information and developing skills as and when needed. They set their own goals, take risks, are resilient and most happy when doing experiments, which primes the brain for spotting opportunities and working smarter.

References

1. Noe, Raymond A. 2010. *Employee Training and Development*, 5th ed. New York: McGraw-Hill.
2. Gruber, M. J., B. D. Gelman and C. Ranganath. 2014. 'States of Curiosity Modulate Hippocampus-dependent Learning via the Dopaminergic Circuit'. *Neuron*, 84(2): 486–496.
3. Dhamija, Anshul. 2013, 22 May. Phaneesh Murthy Rises from Ashes to Bite Dust Again. *The Economic Times*. Available at https://economictimes.indiatimes.com/tech/ites/phaneesh-murthy-rises-from-ashes-to-bite-dust-again/articleshow/20190105.cms (accessed 8 February 2018).

4. Bhattacharya, Saumya. 2011, 21 August. Management Lessons: Treat Your Failure as Valuable Feedback. *The Economic Times.* Available at https://economictimes.indiatimes.com/management-lessons-treat-your-failure-as-valuable-feedback/articleshow/9677031.cms (accessed 8 February 2018).

5. Abidi, Suhayl. 2012, 16 April. Continuous Learning in a Turbulent World. *Business Standard.* Available at http://www.business-standard.com/article/management/continuous-learning-in-a-turbulent-world-1120416 00053_1.html (accessed 8 February 2018).

6. Swallow, Erica. 2012, 25 April. Creating Innovators: Why America's Education System Is Obsolete. *Forbes.* Available at https://www.forbes.com/sites/ericaswallow/2012/04/25/creating-innovators/#3fff59797202 (accessed on 8 February 2018).

7. Wagner, Tony. 2008. *The Global Achievement Gap.* New York: Basic Books.

8. American Management Association. 2012. *Critical Skills Survey.* Available at http://playbook.amanet.org/wp-content/uploads/2013/03/2012-Critical-Skills-Survey-pdf.pdf (accessed 8 February 2018).

9. Office of Disability Employment Policy. *Skills to Pay the Bills.* Department of Labor, United States. Available at https://www.dol.gov/odep/topics/youth/softskills/softskills.pdf (accessed 8 February 2018).

10. Yosida, S. 1989. *Quality Improvement and TQC Management at Calsonic in Japan and Overseas.* Paper presented at Second International Quality Symposium, Mexico.

11. Harris, Breanne. 2015, 9 September. *The Status of Critical Thinking in the Workplace.* Pearson TalentLens. Available at https://www.pearsoned.com/the-status-of-critical-thinking-in-the-workplace/ (accessed 8 February 2018).

12. Prasad, Rachita. 2017, 23 August. Could've Been Conservative, But in 2008–09 Everyone Was Chasing Growth: Prashant Ruia. *The Economic Times.* Available at https://economictimes.indiatimes.com/news/company/corporate-trends/couldve-been-conservative-but-in-2008-09-everyone-was-chasing-growth-prashant-ruia/articleshow/60182484.cms (accessed 8 February 2018).

13. *The Economist.* 2017, 29 June. What Rosneft's Purchase of Essar's Oil Refinery Means: The Chastening of an Indian Conglomerate. Available at https://www.economist.com/news/business/21724444-chastening-indian-conglomerate-what-rosnefts-purchase-essars-oil-refinery-means (accessed 8 February 2018).

14. Press Trust of India. 2017, 16 December. Sunil Mittal Regrets 'Rushed' Decision to Venture Into Africa. *Business Standard.* Available at http://www.business-standard.com/article/companies/sunil-mittal-regrets-rushed-decision-to-venture-into-africa-117121501366_1.html (accessed 8 February 2018).

15. Colvin, Geoffrey. 2001, 8 January. Changing of the Guard; Some People Think Jack Welch is Irreplaceable. Not Welch. Here is the Inside Story of How He and the GE Board Selected His Successor. *Fortune Magazine.* Available at http://archive.fortune.com/magazines/fortune/fortune_archive/2001/01/08/294478/index.htm (accessed 8 February 2018).

16. Wagner, Tony. 2008, October. 'Rigor Redefined'. *Educational Leadership*, 66(2): 20–25.

17. Carr, Austin. 2013, 2 November. Nike: The No. 1 most Innovative Company of 2013. *Fast Company.* Available at https://www.fastcompany.com/3005275/nike-2 (accessed 8 February 2018).

18. Denning, Steve. 2015, 13 March. How Agile and Zara are Transforming the US Fashion Industry. *Forbes.* Available at

https://www.forbes.com/sites/stevedenning/2015/03/13/
how-agile-and-zara-are-transforming-the-us-fashion-
industry/#11f369f27e82 (accessed 8 February 2018).

19. Aspiring Minds. 2016. *National Employability Report (Engineers)*. Available at http://www.aspiringminds.com/
sites/default/files/National%20Employability%20
Report%20-%20Engineers%20Annual%20Report%20
2016.pdf (accessed 8 February 2018).

20. Rowling, J. K. 2008, 5 June. Text of J. K. Rowling's Speech. *The Harvard Gazette*. Available at https://news.harvard.edu/gazette/story/2008/06/text-of-j-k-rowling-speech/ (accessed 8 February 2018).

21. Pucher, Max J. 2011, 24 October. *The Value of Failure*. Available at https://isismjpucher.wordpress.com/2011/10/24/the-value-of-failure/ (accessed 8 February 2018).

22. Kristof, Nicholas. 2016, 4 June. Meet Sultana, the Taliban's Worst Fear. *The New York Times*. Available at https://www.nytimes.com/2016/06/05/opinion/sunday/meet-sultana-the-talibans-worst-fear.html (accessed 8 February 2018).

Chapter 6
The World Is Your Classroom: Self-learning Tools

Give me six hours to chop down a tree and I will spend the first four sharpening the axe.

—Abraham Lincoln

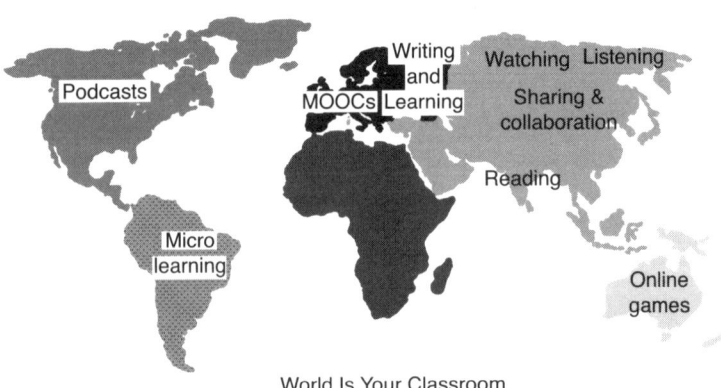

World Is Your Classroom

Today, we live in the golden age of self-learning, surrounded by innumerable tools, starting with the Internet. Who would have ever thought of the latent and explicit power of the Internet and how it has transformed learning around us. The Internet has proven to be the most powerful tool for lifelong learning and its applications are multiplying every day. Soon, the World Wide Web will be supplemented by virtual reality and augmented reality to experience immersive learning. For the curious, there are a variety of options from reading a book, participating in online conversations, collaborating with people throughout the world, writing blogs or having your own website, enrolling in online courses, broadcasting your thoughts, all from the comfort of your laptop and increasingly smartphones. The advantage is that many of these resources are free or very affordable. Have you tried any of these? Supposedly yes! And if not it's not too late. Try getting into elated conversations on blogs and see the transformation.

The advantage of self-learning is that it is on demand and just in time. We can learn what we intend to use, when we want, design our own curriculum and learn at a time and place of our choosing. Companies that deliver effective learning best possess a huge competitive advantage. Effective learning requires that you acquire information through reading, listening, observing, practising, experimenting and experience. One has to soak relevant and meaningful information and develop this acquired information into knowledge and skills, just as Satya Nadella, CEO of Microsoft, did.

> Culture is something that needs to adapt and change, and therefore you've got to be able to have culture to learning. I read a book called Mindset. In there, there's this very simple concept that Stanford Professor Carol Dweck talks about, which is if you take two people, one of them is a learn-it-all and the other one is a know-it-all. In the longer run, the learn-it-all will always trump the know-it-all in the long run, even if they start with less innate capability. [1]

This intuition led to his making 'growth mindset' central to the culture he is trying to change at Microsoft.

Let us take a round of these tools and resources available.

Reading

Whenever I (Abidi) conduct a training programme, the first question I ask is if they have read today's paper. Less than 10 per cent raise their hands. Next, I ask whether they have read any book during the past one month. Again, only one or two participants come forward. The most common excuse is 'Unfortunately, my hectic work schedule leaves me with practically no time at all for reading.' Somewhere along the way, we have lost the reading habit. However, there is one habit common among all great leaders and it is that they are regular readers. Would you believe, as authors, we have read a combined total of over 30 titles in 2017?

Reading is essential for present and prospective leaders and can pay large dividends in the longer run. All top leaders whether Bill Gates, Warren Buffet or Jamie Dimon are voracious readers. Bill Gates once said that he reads at least one book and four to five magazines every month and most of his ideas have come from subjects not related to computers. Jamie Dimon, CEO of JPMorgan, sends lists of books to his staff as suggestions for reading. If you look at the reading list of some of the most respected leaders, you will find that their list is quite broad, not just limited to their work area. How many have you tried until now?

Reading should not be seen as a passive activity, but an active learning process to make connections, understand opinions, research and apply what you learn at your workplace. It is a flexible activity which can be carried out at home, commuting or at vacations. One can read and re-read, search deeper through subject lists and bibliography to get keen insights. Every book or article is written from the writer's perspective, and by going through different materials, we are able to view the world from different perspectives. Even fiction has its uses to understand human emotions, relationships and drivers of action. Books are very versatile, and timeless authors like Peter Drucker can be read and re-read to discover new meaning. There is a philosophy behind each well-crafted writing. The reader must eventually enter into the thoughts and frames of the text and its larger purpose, which at times is not explicit but latent within the writing. One needs to sharpen the skills to understand this hidden treasure of knowledge.

Many out-of-print or free access books including hundreds of classics are available free to download on your Kindle or mobile (e-pub versions).

Many newspapers and magazines such as *Fast Company* provide 'push' newsletters in your mailbox, which you can subscribe for free. Beyond books and magazines, you can subscribe to or visit sites of major business schools such as *Knowledge@Wharton* or HBS Working Knowledge to study their latest offerings. Most business consultants such as McKinsey & Company, Bain & Company and Deloitte too have learning sites where their latest articles and research findings are published.

For busy persons or those who would like to sample a bite before committing extensive time to reading, there are publishers who send book summaries, such as www.summaries.com. These offerings get you ideas and know-how from an entire business book in 10 per cent of the cost and 5 per cent of the time. Try this!

Today, much of the world's publishing from newspapers to books and magazines are also available through mobile applications. Audio recordings of many books and summaries too are available for ease of learning.

Mentor Box

This is a new and unique learning platform built around books. It brings key insights from books through videos, audios and summaries, and you can actively learn using workbooks. The online subscription, which is quite reasonable at $7 per month (or $59 annually) gives you access to over 500 courses. The more expensive physical subscription which costs $139 per month brings you a personally curated educational box every month with two books (print copy), video programs with the authors of the books on a USB stick, workshops, summaries in print and audio. All designed to help you quickly absorb and then retain the concepts of each box. The boxes also include a bibliography of additional reading on the subject to encourage the reader who wishes to dig deeper.

Watching and Listening

Next to reading and learning convenience is watching movies, documentaries and video clips, much of it free of cost. For example, the movie *The King's Speech* is about King George VI of England who stuttered and consequently, due to fear of ridicule, resisted public speaking. It is an important lesson in leadership that you succeed when you let go of your ego. In this case, King George VI was able to overcome his serious disability which interfered with his official duties when he changed his mindset from king to a pupil. It also teaches resilience that you grow stronger as you overcome adversity. How many of us are ready to introspect and shed our ego, which is detrimental to continuous learning?

Guru Dutt's *Sahib, Bibi Aur Ghulam*, an Indian movie classic, too has a profound message for all times that those who cling to the past and do not change with time lose everything and simply vanish. Likewise, *Scent of a Woman* is a story of two failures who help each other raise themselves out of their hopeless situations. A lesson in interdependence. Start thinking now!

YouTube, with its millions of video recordings, most of these free of cost, is another very rich source of learning on any topic about almost anything. One very inspiring content on YouTube is the TED series talks. TED stands for technology, entertainment, design and brings world's leading academics, teachers and innovators to share their thoughts in easily absorbable, short talks.

Besides YouTube, thousands of documentaries in various subjects such as psychology, biography, nature, etc., are streaming free at sites such as Top Documentaries, SnagFilms, etc. Their applications can be downloaded on smartphone and viewed 'on the go'.

YouTube EDU is Google's YouTube education channel. A large number of educational contents such as lectures and conference talks are available here.

The DO Lectures inspires talks from disrupters and change agents, enemies of status quo.

Fora.TV has a large and expanding collection of videos from the world's biggest conferences and events on hot topics of today.

Talks at Google is a Google programme where innovators, thinkers and doers visit Googleplex regularly to give inspiring talks, which are posted freely online by Google.

CreativeLive is an online education platform where live workshops are taught by world-class experts and are free if you mark the talks on your schedule and watch the live streams.

Reddit Lectures includes video lectures on topics worldwide.

Watch streaming documentaries as they bring the real world to learners and ignite curiosity. They expand our world and introduce us to struggles, innovation, empathy and values. After viewing and discussing a film, learners are prompted to see the same view from different perspectives, assisting them in integrating knowledge from various points of view and applying these new ideas. Some of the top documentary films sites are Top Documentary Films and Documentary Heaven.

Podcasts
Another form of passive learning is to listen to podcasts, which are recorded talks or conversations available from a variety of sources such as Ted Talks, Podcasts and Radiolab.

Micro Learning
We all have short gaps in our schedule or downtime when we are commuting or waiting at stations and airports. You can recharge yourself with micro learning, short burst of information to be absorbed within minutes. You can learn German one word per day at *Your Daily German.* These 'bite-sized' snacks ensure that you can absorb information quickly and efficiently, on the go, on any device mobile or the web. Cudcoo is one such online company which has hundreds of courses, priced $2.99 to $4.99, the price of a coffee latte while Inshorts, an Indian company, gives you every news in 60 words or less on your mobile.

Online Courses
Massive Open Online Courses is a recent development which allows unlimited enrolment to online courses. The

website www.mooc-list.com aggregates these courses from worldwide sources.

There are several education companies that are large selection of online courses which you can complete at your pace. There are both free and fee-based courses. We suggest that first you sample the free offerings before spending your hard-earned money. Of course, many of the free programmes do not give a certificate at the conclusion. We too have tried and had great inspiring takeaways. Learning itself was its own certification motivating us to explore further.

Lynda is a virtual paradise for learning and once you connect yourself to people of your choice, you can share a regular stream of tips, summaries, links to articles, reports and even job offerings as well as converse with them. Lynda is the online education platform of LinkedIn with over 6,000 fee-based courses in business, technology and creative skills.

Coursera is the largest fee-based course platform for massive open online courses (MOOCs) with over 25 million students around the world.

Udacity focuses on STEM (science, technology, engineering, mathematics) disciplines.

edX, founded by Harvard University and MIT in 2012, is an online learning destination and MOOC provider, offering high-quality courses from 90 global partners, many of them with high QS ranking such as Berkeley, Columbia, Caltech, etc. This learning resource was founded by and continue to be governed by colleges and universities. It is the only leading MOOC provider that is both non-profit and open source. There are over 10 million learners and 1,300+ courses worldwide. Open edX is the open-source platform that powers edX courses and is freely available.

MIT OpenCourseWare is an initiative to make available all of undergraduate and graduate course materials freely available on the web for anyone, anywhere. This has inspired more than 250 other institutions to do the same.

Khan Academy is a not-for-profit online academy, whereby expertly created courses are available on the web for anyone to learn many academic subjects, including Indian curriculum maths. The software identifies strengths and learning gaps. The Academy has also partnered with institutions such as NASA, the Museum of Modern Art, the California Academy of Sciences and MIT to offer specialized content.

Saylor Academy is a non-profit organization that provides free open courses for everyone.

Udemy covers over 55,000 courses on digital skills.

And the list is countless. Skills transformation cannot be attained without a systematic approach, and traditional degrees are no longer enough to keep up with the pace. Udacity, an online education company, offers nanodegree programmes in areas such as self-driving cars, AI, machine learning, robotics, and mobile and web development, and it's becoming a popular micro-credential option.

The HyperLearning Toolkit designed by Kyle Pierce (www.diygenius.com) is an excellent place to start learning using a structure to design your own learning using the Internet. Its contents include 21st-century reading list of books, documentaries, digital skills, applications, virtual reality and augmented reality, etc. A major reason that many people fail in online learning is because learning a new skill is difficult and it requires a lot of focus and determination to succeed, especially when you are pursuing it on your own. You have to be passionately motivated, define clear goals for learning and draw a self-directed learning plan. This website provides tools and suggestions to do that.

Online Games, Virtual Reality and Augmented Reality

In addition to absorbing information from books and video contents, we can immerse ourselves in a digital world. Environments that we can interact with and explore autonomously could make educational content as engaging as video games. This is a new learning tool and still in developmental stage. Still many platforms are available to engage learners such as Google Expeditions and Discovery VR. However, you have to invest in a good headset.

Online games like the following allow you to develop real-life skills:

1. EVE Online: This provides a practice on running the most powerful company in the world. This may lead to sharpening one's skills for management in the real world.
2. Ports of Call: This long running game has a 3D facelift. Try playing this game to build your shipping fleet wisely and then learn plenty about economics while playing.

Sharing and Collaboration

Everyone has something to learn, and everyone has something to teach. Passive individual learning can only take you so far. For real learning, we need other curious people around us who can challenge our thinking, provide different perspectives, help each other solve problems and jointly develop innovative ideas. Through collaborative learning, one retains information longer and fosters creative thinking. Some important collaboration sites are:

Quora: Seek crowdsourced advice on every possible topic.

Scribd: This is a library of digital documents on every subject. Share your documents and let your creativity be known to the world.

SlideShare: Share power point presentations on every imaginable topic.

G Suite: The best online collaboration suite for cloud productivity.

MindMeister: An online mind-mapping tool that lets you capture, develop and share ideas visually. It is suitable for brainstorming, note taking, project planning and many other creative tasks. Collaborators can quickly comment on topics, vote on ideas or discuss changes.

Creative Commons: This provides free, easy-to-use copyright licenses to make a simple and standardized way to give the public permission to share and use your creative work.

Connexions: This is an open source learning system. View, share and reuse free educational material in small modules that can be organized as courses, books, reports or other academic assignments.

Writing for Learning

Beyond improving communication skills, writing is the highest form of learning where your distilled thoughts are taken to a larger audience. We can only write passionately and convincingly about things we believe in. We create white papers, articles, blogs, webinars and videos. Our words have the power to persuade people to take action. Have you ever tried writing based on your experience? You can even start writing a diary to reflect on your actions. It is a very powerful tool in reminiscing, acknowledging and learning from one's own journey.

The greatest leaders do not just have in-depth knowledge about their own sphere of work but possess knowledge on a variety of subjects. They apply knowledge from different subjects to solve problems. Warren Buffet advocates reading 500 pages a day because that's how knowledge builds up like compound interest, and Harry Truman said, 'not all readers are leaders, but all leaders are readers'. We, as authors, we have written articles in management journals with ideas and examples taken from subjects such as physics, astronomy, wildlife, biology, adventure, natural disasters, history, psychology, to name a few, that have strengthened our belief in universal learning. Even browsing comic characters such as Tintin and Asterix has enabled our adventurous learning terrain even more exciting. Meeting kids and getting exposed to newer sets of information and perspectives, as they expose a breadth and depth of diverse information, is the most powerful element in our learning journey. The young minds are ahead of their time in thoughts and imagination. Learning is like the real universe, limitless and ever-expanding.

You are the most valuable asset you possess, and you should invest continuously in your career and professional achievements. Any investment you make in yourself will multiply many times over in your career and life, and lead to overall success. Even on days when you are very busy, spare a few minutes to your learning. This investment will give you maximum returns.

Reference

1. Bass, Dina. 2016, 4 August. *Satya Nadella Talks Microsoft at Middle Age*. Bloomberg. Available at https://www.bloomberg.com/features/2016-satya-nadella-interview-issue/ (accessed 8 February 2018).

Chapter 7
Together We Learn; Together We Grow

Alone we are smart
Together we are brilliant

—Steven Anderson

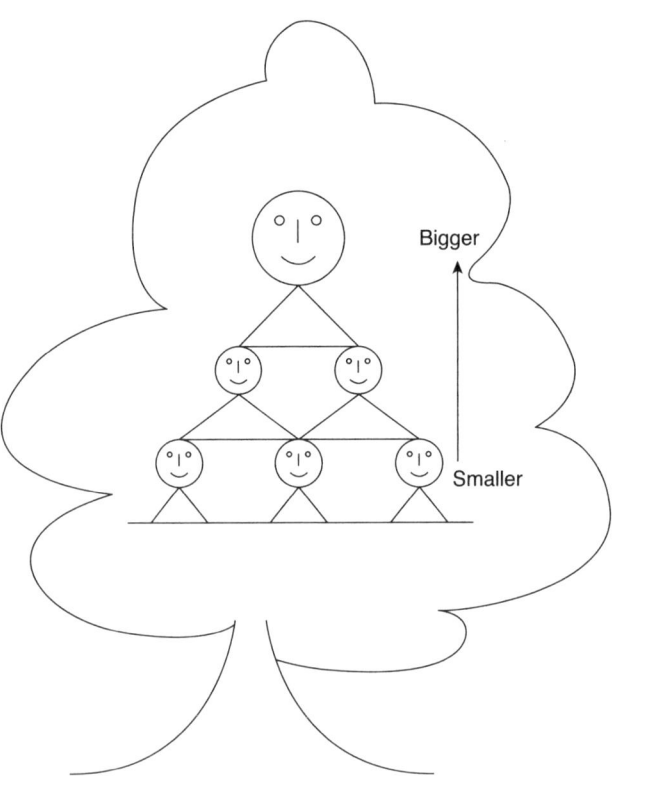

Together We Learn; Together We Grow

Humans are social animals. Our ancestors who lived in hunter-gatherer society learnt through observation, listening and participation. Everybody did everything from making tools to hunting to gathering berries and other food. Knowledge was shared freely and activities like storytelling and dancing appeared to transfer knowledge to next generations. With the advent of agricultural societies, specialization started appearing such as potter, carpenter, metal craftsman, etc. Now learning took the shape of apprenticeship where one master craftsman took in several novices who learnt the craft from the teacher over several years. They lived and worked together forming a strong social bond which facilitated learning. This process of learning continued for centuries and came to an abrupt stop with the introduction of Frederick Taylor's principles of scientific management in the early 20th century.

According to one of his principles, the efficiency of each and every person should be taken care of right from his selection. Now work was specialized and divided into two categories. Those who work and those who think. Further, with the introduction of assembly line, work was broken into small segments which required little training to master and the worker spent his/her whole life at the same workstation doing the same repetitive task. A small band of wise men did all the thinking and planning for the growth of the enterprise.

However, the man remained a social animal and though his desire to discover and learn was suppressed through the line and staff organization, it was not totally extinguished. Learning was hardwired in his DNA and whenever an opportunity occurred, man learnt from the shared experiences of his social group. In fact, ability to learn is the only trait which distinguishes us from animals. Today, with the rapid changes taking place in the business environment, we must use all types of learning forms and models to stay abreast of new knowledge and discard the old. Learning from others is one of the most powerful forms of learning where we are participating both as learners and teachers.

Peer Learning

A few years back, in one mega project, the employees found that the project was grinding to a halt due to failure on account of financial closure. They were soon left without work, with eight hours of free time on their hand, lunch, the highlight of the day and the rumour factory blaring at full blast.

Afraid to die of boredom, an idea struck a few. Instead of spending their free time like zombies, six mid-level managers unanimously decided to form a learning group. They decided to meet once a week in a conference room trying to enhance their skills. They ambitiously took on the role of both teachers and learners. Further to this, the group started honing communication skills through presentations and public speaking. What would be the measure of success? It would be the change in Arun's (name changed) communication skills, which the group voted, including Arun, an electrical engineer, to be really atrocious.

Each Wednesday afternoon, in rotation, one participant would take centre stage and steer the group via a presentation on a topic of his interest. The group would then critically review, examine and provide feedback. On hearing of this activity, some more colleagues joined in and the group started soaring. The senior management, on discovering about the activity, initially ridiculed it, but later accepted with understanding. Interestingly, the group deterred any senior colleagues to sit through these learning sessions. This was purely a peer group with no experts on communication skills addressing them.

Six months down the line, the acid test came. Arun's immediate boss who was heading the power plant suffered a massive heart attack, thereby being immobilized for weeks. Arun, his deputy, was asked to temporarily take charge of the department. Interestingly, during this period, several potential investors visited the site and it became mandatory for the facility heads to give presentations followed by question and answers. On one such important visit, incidentally, where promoter directors were also present, Arun made his presentation, confidently followed by his interactions. This was a pleasant surprise for the CEO who was also present. A few months later, the sick head of the department requested premature retirement on account of health, Arun was given a promotion and made the head of power plant project [1]. This is termed as the power of peer learning, where the knowledge resource, its depth and quantum is unmeasurable and immaculate.

Peer learning or learning from your colleagues and friends is a very powerful form of learning. It is a two-way, reciprocal learning activity. Peer learning should be mutually beneficial and involve the sharing of knowledge, ideas and experience between the participants and moving from individual learning to interdependent learning. You learn and also contribute to others' learning. For example, no software professional can survive in his job without support from a peer group where one discusses problem faced in day-to-day operations. With the proliferation of information, no one person possesses the entire knowledge to solve his/her problems and throw half-baked ideas for frank discussions; this becomes more and more important as you rise to the top. The proverb 'Its lonely at the top' has some truth. As the leader rises, he gets surrounded by people who share his beliefs and assumptions, they learn to say things which will please the boss and ultimately there is no one left who can be honest, show a mirror and provide critique.

Many leaders such as CEOs, to get frank advice, share ideas and problems, go out and form or become members of a small group of peers who meet regularly and discuss wide-ranging issues in confidence. Trust is the bedrock here, with the understanding that what is discussed will not go beyond the four walls. In the world today, where technology is increasingly connecting people, information and the world, one feels the need of people around us with whom we can discuss wide-ranging matters, not just visit the narrow alley of your work. The reward can come from the support this group provides. You may already know the answer but the second opinion from people who are not dependent on you can be valuable and they can share advice and encourage risk-taking. Look for people who are different from you demographically, educationally and experience-wise but share same values—people who are good listeners, inquisitive and open to new discoveries. How about you? Stay inquisitive throughout your life.

There are Adobe Learning Groups in Mumbai and other cities. They meet regularly to exchange notes while learning newer software capabilities beyond manuals and the formal training sessions. Adobe regularly interacts with such groups in obtaining insights for upgrading software and manuals. Once, when I (Abidi) interacted with one such group, I was surprised to learn that it was headed by a 15-year-old student.

Indian Institute of Technology, Kharagpur, has been a pioneer in many transformations in the field of engineering academics in India. In a novel initiative to modernize engineering education, IIT Kharagpur introduced peer-assisted learning from 2017 semester. This was an initiative to improve mentorship, coaching, training and tutoring outside the regular classroom set-up for the first year students for the theory subjects with the help of senior students [2]. Teaching is considered one of the highest form of learning, and this would no doubt benefit the seniors too in strengthening their fundamentals. As a bonus, relationships built up during study can extend into their careers.

At HBX, the online initiative at Harvard Business School (HBS) in Boston, Massachusetts, students rely on each other not just to answer questions about the concepts they are studying but also to connect and engage in ways that make them feel a part of something that goes beyond the screens in front of them. There is enough critical mass in a cohort of a few hundred students for individuals to be able to find answers to their questions. Better yet, they can do so without ever having to interact with a teaching assistant (TA) or faculty member—neither of which are even options at HBX. And here's the surprising thing: Students seem to enjoy this process of mutual discovery more than interactions with lecturers [3].

Mentoring

In Greek mythology, Mentor was the son of Alcimus, who appeared in Homer's epic *The Odyssey*. In old age, he was a close friend of Odysseus, who placed upon Mentor the responsibility of his son Telemachus and served as his teacher, while the hero was away fighting at the Trojan War.

Learning from an older and supposedly wiser person is a key aspect of learning and career growth. This is a partnership between two persons, the mentor, usually an experienced person, who shares knowledge, experience, life management tips, advice and support with a younger person called mentee. Mentor is a coach or a guide who helps to enhance the skills, knowledge or work performance of the mentee.

Mentoring relationships are voluntary on both sides and involve the use of skills such as questioning, listening, clarifying and reframing. The mentor also observes the behaviour of the pupil and offers guidance in soft skills. Many companies today provide mentoring programmes using internal or external mentors, especially to those in the middle management who are high performers and have the potential to move to the top management.

Benjamin Graham, known as 'the father of value investing' and author of *The Intelligent Investor*, created and taught many principles of investing safely and successfully that modern investors continue to use today. After reading *The Intelligent Investor*, Warren Buffett applied to Columbia Business School where Graham was a professor. There, Buffett got an opportunity to personally know his idol. Later in the journey, Graham hired Buffett to work at his company. Both of them cemented a strong and everlasting friendship leading to Buffett's extraordinary transformation. 'Ben Graham was certainly the man who set me on the course that's worked now for a good many years', Buffett says [4].

Today, many angel investors not only write cheques for the start-ups but put their expertise in mentoring the new entrepreneurs to avoid pitfalls which are so common in these ventures.

This brings us to a not very popular form of learning, that is, learning from our juniors, also called 'reverse mentoring'. People are hesitant to expose their ignorance in front of their juniors, but even here, a partnership can be formed where both can learn from each other.

My wife (Abidi) is an ophthalmic surgeon. During 35 years we have been married, I have seen her learning at least six different and progressive surgical procedures that have replaced the old in cataract surgery. During each change, the surgeon must take time off and learn the new technique. Over a period of time, my wife became professor and head of the department of ophthalmology at a medical college, and with other institutional responsibilities, she could not leave her work for an extended period to learn the latest technique. She found a way out. She had an opening for an assistant professor and she chose a young surgeon who came highly recommended for the new cataract technique. She asked him to teach her and other surgeons in the department the new technique and once this phase was over, she sent him to a sister medical college to teach them too. In this way, she learnt from a person at least 20 years junior to her. What was the reward for the new surgeon in sharing his skills? He learnt how to manage complicated and rare cases, knowledge of which is acquired from long experience. Therefore, keeping the pride aside, both learnt from each other.

I have often seen grandparents asking their grandchildren how to operate WhatsApp and Skype. They have no shame in learning from the very young and if we show humility, we can also learn from our juniors. Knowledge is not the exclusive property of position or seniority but is widespread and we should learn to leverage it from whatever the source.

Networking

We are members of one or more networks which exist within the workplace and outside, especially face-to-face groups such as reading groups and social networks such as LinkedIn and Facebook which are built on crowdsourcing principles, rather than face-to-face interactions. Today, many intelligence alerts about new jobs and openings are passed through these social networks, and even organizations are learning to tap into these networks for their job requirements.

When I was working, about once a week I used to meet with Kaushal, a colleague of mine, for about half an hour updating myself on company information and matters. The company was undergoing a rapid change and I, thus, required information not necessarily passed on through official channels. Kaushal had his pulse on whatever was happening with a vast well-placed network of colleagues across departments. These networks had been built up over a number of years on a mutual sharing and learning basis. He offered powerful insights into management's decisions built on the information gleaned from his network. Once, he told me that the ongoing internal restructuring points to the sale of parts of the company in the near future. It turned out that company sold a major part of its operations to a multinational after three years.

He was also my first point of inquiry whenever there was a need for introduction to an unknown person or on understanding procedures and processes. He was an integral part of the social network, which was essential to my work and I assiduously cultivated this precious web [5].

A personal learning network is one of the most powerful forms of keeping abreast of new knowledge, developing joint insights, finding answers to problems and finding entrepreneurial opportunities. It is one of the seven critical skills for survival and sustainable career. In a VUCA world, where information is exploding exponentially, a network which filters, validates, selects and edits appropriate information within a context will become vital for our lifelong professional growth. Over time, you will learn how to attract quality people to your group and how to join such a quality group. This requires patience. The group or groups you join may consist of both a shared discipline and across disciplines. It may be necessary to meet occasionally or often in person to develop strong bonds.

Networking is not just a trend, a fad that will die out soon enough. The success of Facebook, Twitter and LinkedIn is not simply a result of computer and connectivity technology but they replicate what biology already knows. Our DNA too is a network and so is chemistry.

Alumni Network

Peer learning is taken a step forward by leveraging the alumni network of your class whether high school, engineering college or business school which is one of the most powerful and enduring network you can be part of. For learning, job hunting, mentorship, introductions and support, this is an invaluable ally. A class of 30 with their respective first level networks can raise your level of contacts five times and above.

Networking Outside the Organization

Learning is a varied, multi-access activity that we need to learn rapidly and continuously in order to appreciate and foster knowledge in all its variations and diversity. Learners not only share knowledge and skills with homogeneous groups but widen their horizon of learning by sharing knowledge with people with heterogeneous skills and interests. Different people with their unique background can bring different perspectives and enliven the transaction and discussions.

We should never miss an opportunity when attending conferences, workshops or other external events to widen our network.

The next step in network learning is collaboration. Open source development of Wikipedia and open Linux have demonstrated the capability of learning and action when individuals work together in groups. The number of applications in Linux is already many times more than the proprietary, control-freakish environments of Apple and Microsoft. File-sharing applications on cloud, and easy and cheap online conferencing are facilitating the learning environment of networks.

GenHERation, started by a Wharton graduate, is a network which develops leadership skills in women through support, knowledge sharing and collaboration. This network exposes about 250 young women in the United States to leadership opportunities. Every week, one company challenges the girls to solve a real-life problem, such as creating a marketing strategy to help a bank reach young women or creating product packaging for a toy company. With demonstrated success stories, companies were willing to pay for these research insights, and also these companies were willing to pay to recruit young talent to their companies. This programme created an inexpensive, more effective way to reach young, ambitious women. The women come from all socio-economic backgrounds and aspire to be everything from nurses to engineers. The one thing they share is ambition. Initially, the Wharton alumni provided critical introductions to companies that become clients. In turn, those highly satisfied clients have provided additional referrals to GenHERation [6].

Access to the widespread Internet allows large numbers of people to share information and solicit feedback instantaneously and at little cost. In fact, the Internet has been found useful in research where academics now can easily share and validate their data. Software professionals have long been using the Internet to connect to each other to solve coding problems, understand manuals, which generally are not very user-friendly, seek jobs and otherwise engage with their colleagues in a fast-changing technology and knowledge environment.

Social Media

We now have the tools such as LinkedIn, Twitter and Facebook where we can leverage learning groups with members from around the globe. Even for people with very specialized skills or needs, you can always find a few people throughout the world who share your area of knowledge.

For many people, Twitter terminology can get bewildering but with patience, you can learn these. You need not be introduced to anyone on Twitter. If you find any person or organization interesting, you can just start following their outputs. Once you start commenting, or start your own conversation, you can discover people with whom you can have stimulating discussion and find new resources. One advantage of Twitter is that it teaches you to be brief, an important skill in a VUCA world.

By harnessing the power of the LinkedIn groups, you can tap into an expansive network of professionals and groups in your discipline and beyond, share updates, find new career opportunities and contribute your own thought leadership. Writing on LinkedIn allows you to develop a following, demonstrate expertise in your field and connect with new opportunities—all on a scale never before possible. Once you're a group member, you can explore the latest conversations on the conversations page, start or participate actively in conversations and send a message to a member if you want to reach out to them. There are upwards of 2.5 million groups on LinkedIn and you are sure to find a few which you would like to join and contribute.

Similarly, Facebook can be used by the group to share resources, fire up discussions and promote collaboration using a range of multimedia tools such as videos, images, boards, chatting and private messaging. The learning possibilities are only limited by your imagination.

We are moving towards an interdisciplinary and collaborative ideology of knowledge creating and learning environments addressing problems that are multidimensional and complex. The resolution cannot be the territory of a single discipline. Doctors are learning that many diseases such as diabetes require management through interdisciplinary approach such as endocrinology, nephrology, ophthalmology, dietary science, etc., which can provide improved level of care to the patient.

Knowledge consists of 'know why' and 'know how'. Networks help us in breaching both bastions. From who is teaching whom, we are now shifting to who is learning from whom. Even where one is learning in isolation through offline and online tools, we still need networks for the deepening and embedding of our knowledge. Networks are a core source of intellectual energy for igniting creativity and extending the circulation of ideas and practices. They further are responsible for engaging each one of us in sustained innovative activities while increasing the confidence in facing newer challenges. The connectivity provided by digital devices and networks allows us to expand each other's contribution and continuously expand our knowledge horizon.

References

1. Abidi, Suhayl. 2012, 16 April. Continuous Learning in a Turbulent World. *Business Standard.* Available at http://www.business-standard.com/article/management/continuous-learning-in-a-turbulent-world-112041600 053_1.html (accessed 8 February 2018).

2. Indian Institute of Technology, Kharagpur. *New Learning Methods.* Available at http://alumni.iitkgp.ac.in/content/new-learning-methods (accessed 8 February 2018).

3. Mullane, Patrick. 2017, 31 August. The Wisdom of Peers. *BizEd.* Available at http://bized.aacsb.edu/articles/2017/09/the-wisdom-of-peers (accessed 8 February 2018).

4. Mejia, Zameena and Kathleen Elkins. 2017, 29 September. Warren Buffett Credits His Success to These 3 People. *CNBC.* Available at https://www.cnbc.com/2017/09/29/warren-buffett-credits-his-success-to-these-3-people.html (accessed 8 February 2018).

5. Abidi, Suhayl. 2001, 18 September. The Social Life of LAN. *Business Standard,* Available at http://business-standard.com/strategist/guestcolumn30.asp?menu= (accessed 8 February 2018).

6. Stengel, Geri. 2017, 13 September. How A Strong College Network Opens Doors for Young Women. *Forbes.* Available at https://www.forbes.com/sites/geristengel/2017/09/13/how-a-strong-college-network-opens-doors-for-young-women/#317aab1c2e26 (accessed 8 February 2018).

Chapter 8
Family Firm Scion: Learning in the Family Business

The pessimist complaints about the wind, the optimist expects it to change, the realist adjusts the sail.

—William A. Ward

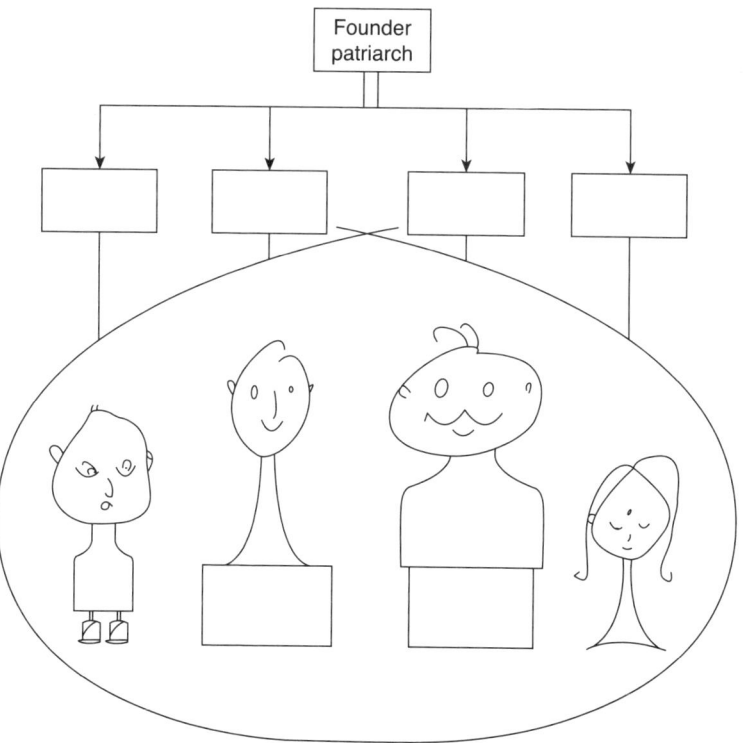

Learning from the Family Business

It is generally assumed that in a fast-moving VUCA (volatility, uncertainty, complexity, ambiguity) environment, family businesses would have difficulty in sustaining their survival and growth, but we believe that wanting the business to succeed in the long run makes it easier for family enterprises to leave aside strategy which offers short-term gains.

Many professional CEOs, heading such giants as BP and Rio Tinto, have delivered long-term blow to their companies by focusing on short-term objectives which is generally linked to their bonus. Tony Hayward at BP, in his speed to take BP to no. 2 position in the oil industry from then no. 7, took decisions which have so far led to estimated $50 billion in fines and costs and over 50 per cent erosion in market value. Today, BP is at no. 17. Much has been written about how Richard Fuld, keeping as the focus solely on the bottom line (and his linked bonus), took Lehman Brothers down the road to bankruptcy. Family concerns, as they are not overly concerned with quarterly results, can forgo short-term gains for longevity. This makes them more resilient to ups and downs of the marketplace. In fact, research has shown that family firms do better than companies with dispersed ownership during a recession.

Family firms make up the majority of companies in the world, with places such as the Middle East and Asia, including India, primarily driven by family businesses. More than 30 per cent of large corporations such as Walmart, Samsung, Cargill Foods, Gap and Ford are family controlled. In India, Tata, Bajaj and Mahindra are household names. The family-managed companies account for more than 30 per cent of all companies with sales in excess of $1 billion, according to the BCG's analysis. 'This is the model for the 21st century', says Randal Carlock, co-author of *When Family Businesses are Best* and a family enterprise professor at the INSEAD School of Business in France. Many companies have built up decades' worth of collective knowledge about what it means to run a business—any business, big or small.

In the 21st-century model of the company, resilience is the foremost quality, which should be developed within a leader. Agility and adaptability, the other two character-istics, which determine success in a VUCA environment, cannot be brought into action unless the firm survives. In a VUCA environment, failures are frequent and resilience, the characteristic of bouncing back from failure, should be built into the leader's DNA.

According to a research study published in *Harvard Business Review*, family businesses focus on resilience more than performance. They forgo the excess returns available during good times in order to increase their odds of sur-vival during bad times. This is a sound strategy for VUCA times where future changes fast and moves in directions you never imagined [1].

Havells' acquisition of the much larger German com-pany Sylvania reflects both the resilience and long-term strategy, which prevails in a well-run family business. The takeover did not proceed well and Sylvania went into losses during the 2008 recession, hammering down Havells' share value to a third. Many bankers advised the promoter late

Qimat Rai Gupta to take a loss and sell the acquired company. A professional CEO with an eye on the quarterly results would have done so, but not Gupta. He took the challenge to turn around the company head on.

Gupta confronted his son and nephew, his two lieutenants. He told them in no uncertain terms that Havells has received a big setback after the acquisition. Sylvania's poorly performing balance sheet is a blow to Havells' reputation. If they fail to turn around the acquired company, no banker would have confidence in their competence and this would put a stop to any future acquisition. This was not only a big challenge but an opportunity to prove their merit.

Over the next few months, the duo concerted together and consolidated operations in South America and downsized the Europe business. They further relocated the nerve centre to Noida from New York and migrated the production to low-cost manufacturing set-ups in China and India. By 2010, Sylvania had turned the corner [2].

Extensive research on family business reveals that 'family' is all about 'emotions', while 'business' is about 'economics'. It is difficult to separate them and at the same time is complementary to the performance and existence of a family business. An imbalance can lead to discord or harmony in the business. A very recent Indian example is the succession of Ratan Tata at Tata Sons, which is controlled by a family trust of the Tata family. The Group had a succession issue that was resolved with a complex yet strategically driven initiative by its ex-chairman. This is an evidence of earlier decisions to keep control over the family business; there was a trade-off between choosing competence and a family member (even if it was a distant one). Trust issues and imbalances in a large group with empowered leadership at all levels versus centralization of decision-making at group level provided a great amount of learning in a family business. This is just one example. The crux lies in 'keeping the business in the family' and the 'family in the business'.

Family business as a general understanding has three main components, namely, ownership, family and management, with the prime purpose of keeping wealth, family and business intact. There has to be a careful selection between the choices amongst these components while strategic decisions are crafted and executed. At times when familiness prevails during the transition of the family business, conflicts surround ownership leading to conflicts and disharmony in the family business. This may finally lead to the erosion of the business and wealth, followed by a split between the members of the family.

Research on family business has evolved globally and therefore it is important to understand and examine the factors that influence family-owned and family-managed businesses. Widely it is learnt that the most daunting task with the family business owners is to manage the responsibilities between the family and the family business. Priorities can take a shift but the central issue revolves around keeping the family intact, the growth of business and maximization of wealth [3].

So what do you think can really assist? Is the correct identification of priorities within the family and business, the right assorted strategies, optimized utilization of resources and capabilities and their balance the right answer? Generically, power struggles, succession planning, conflicts and their mitigation, governance, etc., are fairly complex dimensions that are intertwined and affect the decision process in a family business.

The main challenge in operating a family business is between the concerns for the family vis-à-vis for the business. Every family business has its own complex dimensions, which can be termed as peculiar to its kind and has no fixed solutions. It is, therefore, as a learning, necessary to understand the culture around decision-making, which imparts greater value to the family business. Aggressiveness, fearlessness and competition among the owners of the family business and other members are very natural. Therefore, the governance structure and the process of decision-making needs to be clearly understood in a family business, which may be unique to each one.

Nonaka's theory of knowledge creation and conceptualization of a knowledge-creating place has tried to address our learning on succession. According to him, 'Ba' is a perception of a place, which is the family business and a shared purpose among the family members. In many family firms, especially where promoters and potential successors live in a joint family, there is a great deal of ceremony attached to all members being present at dinner time. In an informal atmosphere where many generations could be present, matters are discussed and concerns aired in an informal setting. Many young family members, who may still be in school, observe the process of knowledge transfer and conflict resolution at the dinner table. This is a form of 'Ba' where individuals transcend one's own limited perspective or boundary. In other family firms such as Havells, the first hour in the morning is set aside for the meeting of the management which may consist of both family members as well as professional managers.

If 'Ba' is absent, there can be a considerable amount of tension and barriers in the succession process. Therefore, a family business must create a 'Ba' which is essential to its survival [4]. The knowledge of the family business and its members within the family becomes crucial and impacts on succession. Is there a formal understanding or process of creating a succession strategy? If there is, then how is it transited? There is an immense learning that can take place even by questioning oneself as to what is the significant difference in succession strategies based on the nature and type of knowledge possessed by a family business. Do family businesses append their knowledge dynamically to a viable succession process? How is tacit and explicit knowledge exploited in keeping the family and business intact?

There is an ongoing challenge in keeping the business in the family and the family in the business, which can be classified as a legacy issue [5]. The question that is uppermost is whether the family (and the family business) is interested in developing its members in keeping pace with changing needs of a complex business environment. There are emotional and power-related issues that plague the family businesses. It is, however, clear that business desires the best out of its people particularly from the family members in order to ensure maximum and optimum results.

Family businesses around the world have different values and beliefs [6]. There is a significant difference between the members of the family business and the professionals who do not come from the family. Culturally if one dissects, there is a big difference. The members may or may not have ownership but are inclined to keep the family business rolling, while the employed professional focuses upon the business and not the family. For the professional, though succession may be an important decision for the family business' survival, in the long run, the focus is on maximization of business revenues, as a bottom line. Thus, heirship may be important but not critical as an operation in a VUCA business environment.

Differentiation as a competitive advantage is of prime concern in a family business [7]. Firms compete on differentiation in the race for existence. But it has to be sustainable. We understand that the family businesses represent a large share as in by small firms in major economies around the world. Having in mind the global economic situation, this trend is expected to continue. Members of the family with a high level of locus of control have a general feeling of they being important elements in the decision-making process. At times, due to the web in familiness, they feel trapped in individual decision-making, as it is felt around that decisions are by and for the family in the family business. There is a strong possibility of successors being hit by this dilemma.

There could be diverse views and, as a result, the potential successors might choose a different career progression, away from the core family business, where the locus of control is higher due to independence. How to make the firm competitive may be one of the important decisions that might plague the family and the business, with younger incumbents being left out of the discussions and decisions. Thus, comparable with a high locus of control, individuals with increased self-efficacy will have the propensity to choose succession rather than start a new business. There is an immense amount of complexity and ambiguity within the family business, which needs clarity.

The fallout between Qimat Rai Gupta and his eldest son, Ajesh, who was the heir apparent of Havells, due to their contrasting operating styles and dual centres of power that created leadership confusion, is a constant reminder of the succession conflicts, which can emerge in a family firm. The former is not yet ready to hang his boots and the latter is impatient and eager to show his independence [2].

The choice to be or not to be in a family-owned family-controlled business is entirely an individual's choice. The incumbent may like to enter, expand the business or even quit [8]. This is indeed a complex relationship between the past, present and future understanding of the business. It is not simple as said on a choice to stay with the family business or take off as an entrepreneur. However, in both, lifelong learning is to be passionate and risk bearing. While the family business anchors around staying with the family and the business legacy, the latter emphasizes upon self-creation. Motivation levels required by both, that is, the family members and the legacy intended for business are different and at the same time, they intersect too. Values and longevity in a family business are interconnected.

There are values contributing towards family cohesion and firm's sustainability which allow transmission of core values [9].

Let us examine how vision, leadership and EI transform family business. Visionary leadership combined with EI can inspire organizational renewal and the family in business [10]. It's the shared values and emotions, which are very contagious and the leader can use it discreetly towards organizational growth. This at times becomes a part of the family system and its importance must be realized. There must be a fair connect between the family system and the business system. The more the family business progresses towards professionalism, the more the dividend is rewarding for all: to the family, its owners and professionals employed. This professionalism can aid towards the growth of the family, its business and wealth in totality.

Yet succession emerges to be the central issue in a family business and hence there must be some takeaways. Family firms may start with the first generation and may lead to second, third, fourth, etc., and subsequent generations, though there is a strong evidence of firms collapsing from its main course after second and third generations, as we have seen with Mafatlal. The reasons are plenty but lack of succession planning and infusing professionals in the business are some major ones [11]. The transition may or may not be because of assorted reason like the heir being prepared or not prepared in terms of competence required to operate the business. The experience could be another potential factor. In many leading family businesses, the tendency is to introduce the youngsters who might be possible heirs at the entry level. This is to enable the understanding of family business with greater clarity.

If the family values are strong, there is little evidence of sibling rivalry, and the succession transition is smooth and also effective. Formal succession plans may not exist but the family tradition, which is a part of the family system, supports the business culture as an anchor. The planning is more adaptable and agile, and reduces the family dynamics. At times, the formalization process hinders the smooth transition as it may be considered more of a structured way of letting out the baton of ownership. The matters become more complex if an outsider as an advisor is engaged to resolve family matters rather than the family itself. This may further complicate and procrastinate any decision to an uncertainty. A great deal of understanding is desired here to mitigate complexities.

Globally there is an evidence that such transitions happen more smoothly when the heirs are well prepared while the relationship amongst the family members is cordial and based on trust. We must emphasize upon a point stated earlier that it's here that the strong family system, which exists through generations, should hold the pole position. In such cases, the transition is smooth in times of turbulence and uncertainties. The question arises if there is a sibling rivalry in terms of competence and not age or as a natural heir is debated. Do the family relations continue to exist smoothly and not break down eventually? It has been also debated in family business if changing rules due to the transition and succession can affect the existing family and business system. Does it really change from the first to the second, third and subsequent generations? Well, this needs a deeper investigation as it might change over from family to family, geography, culture and the vertical of business.

Entrepreneurial learning in a family business is an important element. Even though family and business overlap, they intersect for their individual existence [12]. In order to foster innovation, knowledge transfer is essential. There should be clarity of understanding between the family members and the key members in the business who may be outside the family. The initiative by youngsters to learn and the experienced or the elders to articulate the learning process must exist. It must be embedded in the DNA of the business. Even though succession may be a micro issue for a family and its business, it may have an everlasting impact on the regional and national economy too, as we have seen with the Ambanis.

The entrepreneurial ability must exist and coexist side by side in the family business. The legacy issue would always be there but if the entrepreneurial ability is absent, the chances of the family business receding in its existence may be high. There must be a mechanism for the subsequent generation to develop and harness entrepreneurial abilities too along with preparations to lead the family business, if not the family. As stated earlier, the interplay between the family system and business system coexists and must be skilfully practised, as in 'Ba' practised in the Japanese culture.

It is well researched that documenting and transferring knowledge whether tacitly or explicitly fuels innovation. This innovation becomes the major tool to survive and perform in a dynamic VUCA world. Thus, there could be situations in which siblings may have to come out of some practices within the family business that are outdated and learn new ones that could sharpen their skills to lead like an entrepreneur. Constant learning and executing as what is optimally desired for the business could deconstruct conflicts necessarily required for the family, business, transferring power and sharing of the wealth.

In a family business, it is critical to understand what a structural crisis and resilience is. Is there an interdependence between cultures and resilience [13] in a family business? There are some cultures around distributed regions in clusters that are spread around the world and have a high level of resilience, a phenomenon which reflects in abilities to return around quickly during difficult times. It has a direct relationship between the entrepreneurial ability, risk-taking propensity and intrinsic motivation to navigate through difficult times. There is a good combination of positive attitude, which is reflected both in an individual's and in a firm's behaviour. Strategic flexibility exists in abundance and this also affects the power or resilience.

Knowledge transfer in a family business foreseeing succession or say transition in family and business is absolutely essential. There are instances when the family undergoes a sudden transition as in the patriarch/owner being incapacitated due to injury, incompetent to handle the dynamic and turbulent challenges, long illness and untimely demise. If knowledge transfer does not take place timely, specifically during the time of founders' existence, the chances of family and its business being affected are very high. The firm may lose its competitive advantage and in the long run may also go down in business and wealth [14]. Can there be a greater amount of cohesion driving the family and its business in a single direction? The family systems and business systems are unique to each firm, culture, region and business, and difficult to replicate. What is important that values of the family get transferred along with the business acumen amongst the successors for the longevity of the business. Therefore, passing the baton [15] requires a successful succession planning which must yield concrete direction to the family and its business.

Hence, we see that there is a strong desire to create a learning organization within a family business [16]. It is understood candidly that without knowledge transfer, a smooth coexistence amongst the family members is not possible. Size of the family business and its members matters but what concerns more is the creation of learning opportunities, which must be continuous. Informal learning or experiential learning is most effective both for personal growth and leveraging the family business. What we emphasize is to have patience for candid and peer review, listening abilities and the power of enquiry. The last one 'enquiry mode' is seriously lagging in the younger generation, and, as a result, most knowledge transfer takes place like a book being transferred, not opened and when required with no clue as to where and how it must be applied. The conundrum of knowledge transfer is high and so are its results: affirmative when there is a mechanism in a family, else the results are disastrous in all modes of transition.

So what do we see in future? The business environment in the current context has become more volatile, uncertain, complex and ambiguous. Therefore, it must be analysed both internally and externally for the firm. VUCA also exist in a family business in many forms. There is volatility in changing values, knowledge transfer, EI, successful generations that are much younger, succession process, the business environment, competition, spin-offs, leadership, legacy transfer, role of women, etc. There is an uncertainty in terms of knowledge transfer, succession planning and identifying heirs, conflict resolution, managing sibling rivalry, leadership, etc. The structure of the family and its business must move from complex systems to simple systems. It is said that there is an immense power in simplicity. By simplicity, we imply smoother systems that can coexist in terms of knowledge transfer, balanced EI, the creation of a 'Ba'-like family system, inculcating and transferring values, a well-understood though not always written succession planning, ownership transfer, leadership development and passing over the legacy. Ambiguity must be reduced substantially in order to have a much clearer focused direction for the business.

It is generally presumed that in a dynamic VUCA (volatility, uncertainty, complexity, ambiguity) environment, the family businesses shall undergo challenges for survival and growth simultaneously. They must leave the short-time gains and focus on building a strategy that emphasizes on the strategic intent and sets a direction for long-term gains. There are many examples of CEOs who were focused on short-term gains, which resulted in the downfall of their firms. Many times, family concerns may be procrastinated in the interest of the firm. But stating this may be easy than execution as some family businesses are more oriented and inclined to the family (emotions) than the business (economics). This may be a strategic decision, and, as a trade-off, may require great skills on decision-making, interpersonal skills and handling issues innate to the family and its business.

What should family firms do or undertake to ensure a long-term growth and sustainability? It is well accepted that in a VUCA world, turbulent with disruption around, what worked yesterday might not yield any promising results in the future.

In a VUCA business environment, there is no fixed strategy. In a VUCA world, it is impossible to presume that failures will not strike. What is critical is to possess the resilience to fight back. We introduce the following road map, a possible model for the 21st-century succession planning for the family businesses with next Tata Group succession, as an example, which is likely to come up in about 15 years from now.

Some young Tata family members have recently joined group companies. They must have been distressed to watch their illustrious family name trampled and mauled after the firing of Cyrus Mistry, successor to Ratan Tata as chairman of Tata Sons. It was like watching two hyenas ripping apart a buffalo, which is still breathing. Neither party showed any restraint or humility, which are sterling qualities in a leader.

Now that the scions have joined one of the companies within Tata Group, they must be nursing a hidden desire that someday they would be offered the mantle of leading the Group. It is neither unthinkable nor undesirable, as these children have grown up in an environment, which respects the values that hold the business together.

These scions carry a heavy responsibility on their shoulders simply by surname TATA. They must realize that shoulders muscles must be strengthened from a young age to support the head, which does the thinking, as well as the hands, which do the execution. Learning to both think and execute go side by side.

The aspiration is not misplaced as family members imbibe crucial core values, which anchor the company in times of uncertainty and disruption. The question that comes to mind is what can be done in terms of succession planning in family businesses so as to ensure its long-term growth and sustainability. In a fast-moving and disruptive world where following yesterday's practices of rotation and tutelage under a mentor may not be adequate to bring the desired transformation, how do we groom the next generation to play the top role?

The Tata scions have already gone through a privileged education and we assume that they are not in their current jobs as the result of a competitive selection process. Family scions are generally rotated within various departments to get an 'overall learning experience'. Therefore, it can be said that these children have not yet been introduced to hardship, deprivation and failure, which are essential qualities for those who wish to succeed.

Due to a privileged education, they may be in a disadvantageous position to lead in future. People who succeed to the top in a VUCA environment are hungry for success and they reach the top in spite of many odds. This drawback may have contributed to Cyrus Mistry's failure too. Nobody gives them an inch. On this road, failures are many and should be seen as learning pauses. Each failure tests one's resolve to succeed. If one aspires for the top job, peers must say, 'I would like to follow you' and this is exactly what is desired for these incumbents [17].

After a few years in the family business to imbibe the value system, cut your professional teeth outside. It can be a company not linked to your business and today, more likely a start-up. It is seen in many families that scions join consultancy firms to gain experience in strategic thinking. This type of desk assignment can come later in the learning journey.

First, you must get used to the rough and tumble of the marketplace where every day is a struggle to get orders, payments and convince prospects. In short, get blisters on your feet and first toughen your soles. Experience firsthand how wealth is created. Many of today's top entrepreneurs in the pharmaceutical industry started life as a medical representative, such as Ramesh Juneja, founder of Mankind, one of the fastest growing pharmaceutical companies and number five rank in India.

The founder of a Mumbai-based mid-size pharmaceutical company sent his son, after graduation, to work as a medical representative in Assam, the farthest post in the company. For three years, he lived with other medical representatives and rode pillion to visit doctors and chemists, learning how wealth is created at the grassroots level.

According to a story, which appeared in the press recently, in an effort to wean his son from a life of silver-spooned privilege, a Gujarati diamond merchant and proprietor of a Surat-based $1billion company with presence in 71 countries persuaded his only son doing MBA in the United States to go to Kochi incognito and survive on odd jobs for a month.

The father imposed three conditions. For the entire period, he would live only on what he earned and would not touch the money he had taken from home for emergency purposes. He must change his job every week, that is, he cannot work at any one place for more than a week. At last, he could not display his father's identity nor use the mobile phone. The aim was to let his son learn through his struggles, know how poor persons live, get job and money. Do you think any university can teach you these life skills except the first-hand experience?

The son didn't speak Malayalam and after 60 rejections found the first job in a bakery followed by a call centre and a shoe retailer. Where else can you learn resilience? [18].

Humility is the first thing to learn. Only a humble person says that he is ignorant, opening the space for learning.

If you continue to work and grow only in the family company, you are unlikely to get the respect of the millennial, which will form your peer group. This new generation does not respect positions or designations but knowledge and sharing. If you succeed, it would be said that you had family support and if you fail, the same people will call you dumb, who failed in spite of the family support. In either case, you have failed.

To continue on your career graph, you also need a non-family mentor who can provide accurate feedback on performance. Next-generation leaders benefit from knowing how others perceive their leadership behaviour in order to learn the emotional and social skills that account for more than 85 per cent of a top leader's performance. After a decade of work outside, do return to group companies. Now you have gained an outside perspective and a learning mindset, which would allow you to question existing businesses, products, acquisitions, assumptions, beliefs and practices. Question everything. There are no holy cows in business as we were told by the head of a billion-dollar family business that 'I am not in love with any business'.

Mr N. Chandrasekaran, the newly appointed chairman of Tata Sons, is likely to retire in another 15 years. It gives you sufficient time to sharpen your axe. Don't let the current imbroglio in Tata Group deflect you from your path to aim for the top prize.

References

1. Kachaner, Nicholas, George Stalk and Alain Bloch. 2012, November. 'What You Can Learn from Family Business'. *Harvard Business Review*. Available at https://hbr.org/2012/11/what-you-can-learn-from-family-business (accessed 8 February 2018).
2. Bhandari, Bhupesh. 2014, 20 November. Bhupesh Bhandari: The Unsung Billionaire. *Business Standard*. Available at http://www.business-standard.com/article/opinion/bhupesh-bhandari-the-unsung-billionaire-114112001358_1.html (accessed 8 February 2018).

3. Pounder, Paul. 2015. 'Family Business Insights: An Overview of the Literature'. *Journal of Family Business Management* 5 (1): 116–127.

4. Brännback, Malin, Alan Carsrud and William D. Schulte. 2008. 'Exploring the Role of Ba in Family Business Context'. *VINE* 38 (1): 104–117.

5. Tucker, John. 2011. 'Keeping the Business in the Family and the Family in Business: What is the Legacy?' *Journal of Family Business Management* 1 (1): 65–73.

6. Brice, William David and James Richardson. 2009. 'Culture in Family Business: A Two-country Empirical Investigation'. *European Business Review* 21 (3): 246–262.

7. Douglas, Alex, Jacqueline Douglas and John Davies. 2010. 'Differentiation for Competitive Advantage in a Small Family Business'. *Journal of Small Business and Enterprise Development* 17 (3): 371–386.

8. Kjellman, Anders Johan. 2014. 'Family Business Explained by Field Theory'. *Journal of Family Business Management,* 4 (2): 194–212.

9. Tàpies, Josep and María Fernández Moya. 'Values and Longevity in Family Business: Evidence from a Cross-cultural Analysis'. *Journal of Family Business Management* 2 (2): 130–146.

10. Boyatzis, Richard E. and Ceferi Soler. 2012. 'Vision, Leadership and Emotional Intelligence Transforming Family Business'. *Journal of Family Business Management* 2 (1): 23–30.

11. Morris, Michael H., Roy W. Williams and Deon Nel. 1996. 'Factors Influencing Family Business Succession'. *International Journal of Entrepreneurial Behaviour & Research* 2 (3): 68–81.

12. Hamilton, Elenora. 2011. 'Entrepreneurial Learning in Family Business: A Situated Learning Perspective'. *Journal of Small Business and Enterprise Development* 18 (1): 8–26.

13. Ljungkvist, Torbjörn and Börje Boers. 2016. 'Structural Crisis? Regional Culture and Resilience in Family'. *Journal of Enterprising Communities: People and Places in the Global Economy* 10 (4): 425–446.

14. Boyd, Britta, Susanne Royer, Rong Pei and Xiaolei Zhang. 2015. 'Knowledge Transfer in Family Business Successions: Implications of Knowledge Types and Transaction Atmospheres'. *Journal of Family Business Management* 5 (1): 17–37.

15. Drury, Pauline. 2016. 'Passing the Baton: Successful Succession Planning in a Family Business'. *Human Resource Management International Digest* 24 (3): 35–37.

16. Birdthistle, Naomi and Patricia Fleming. 2005. 'Creating a Learning Organization Within the Family Business: An Irish Perspective'. *Journal of European Industrial Training* 29 (9): 730–750.

17. Joshi, Manoj and Suhayl Abidi. 2017, June. 'Winds of Change'. *Indian Management*, 56 (6): 47–49.

18. Sreejith, R. K. 2016, 22 July. Billionaire Dad Sends Son to Kerala to Work as Aam Aadmi. *The Times of India.* Available at https://timesofindia.indiatimes.com/city/kochi/Billionaire-dad-sends-son-to-Kerala-to-work-as-aam-aadmi/articleshow/53327403.cms (accessed 8 February 2018).

Chapter 9

Hierarchy or Wirearchy: Learning in Enterprises

Learning is a process—it is not an event.

—Suzanne Martin, Head of Global People
Development, Google

Learning in Enterprises

There are two things we can say with certainty about the future: it will be different, and it will be full of surprises. This will force you to question your assumptions, beliefs and attitude. This is the VUCA world.

With rapid changes evidenced and anticipated followed by increased competition, the source of economic wealth will be less in the production of material goods but will gravitate towards creation and manipulation of information, knowledge and ideas. This will be the new world. The traditionally accepted competitive edge through products and technology held as pole positions will be short-lived. This is because in the New Age, getting a replica or being replicated with few modifications within a few months should not be a surprise. But on the contrary, people cannot be copied (despite robotic age coming in) and, as a result, their knowledge and professional skills will become the competitive edge.

To compete, all organizations will need knowledge workers. These will be employees whose unmatched talent and experience will be the reason why customers shall approach you instead of the competitors. The effective capabilities in identifying, assimilating, developing, compensating and retaining these talented individuals will be the principal challenge facing all organizations. Now consider how you value knowledge and develop it for a competitive advantage! Have you lost your knowledge base through downsizing? Start introspecting!

The new flatter organizational structures aim to minimize the traditional hierarchy. Therefore, employees are expected to be more self-reliant and hence answerable to customers and demands of the stakeholders. Success was previously measured by the number of steps one would scale up the corporate ladder, whereas today, success is largely measured by the alignment of individual values, the goals and competencies possessed. An individual's competencies must match the changing business needs of the organization.

There is a fallacy in companies that formal processes of training and development contribute to organizational performance, while informal learning is only for individual enrichment. Nothing can be farther from the truth. Today, more than ever, informal learning is taking centre stage due to its flexibility and adaptability to meet fast-changing circumstances. By the time a curriculum is developed and training programme launched, it is already seeing obsolescence. Besides, training and development can only introduce a topic, 'know why' to embed it in individuals, however, one also needs to 'know how' in developing the ability to apply a concept successfully at the workplace. Often, we find that what we have learnt in the classroom needs changes or modification and, in many cases, further clarification to use the acquired knowledge. This requires a workplace where social networks and team working allow us to quickly convert acquired knowledge into revenue streams.

The most important area for development in a VUCA environment is the ability to view the future, candidly and with an open mind.

A Tale of Two Companies: Kodak and Fuji Films

At the peak of its success, by 1976, Kodak enjoyed 90 per cent market share for photographic films and 85 per cent camera sales in the United States with 60 per cent gross margin. Until the 1990s, it was among the five most valuable brands. Fuji Film enjoyed a similar success in Japan. In other markets, they competed fiercely. Today, Kodak is insolvent, while Fuji is thriving.

Both firms saw their traditional business rendered obsolete through the advent of digital photography. But whereas Kodak failed, Fujifilm moved out of the traditional business successfully with a market capitalization of $12.6 billion in 2012 to Kodak's $220 million.

Both saw the inevitable change rushing in! Larry Matteson, a former Kodak executive, recalls writing a report in 1979 mentioning how different parts of the market would switch from film to digital. It started with the government reconnaissance, followed by professional photography and then led the mass market by 2010. He was only a few years out [1].

Success had made Kodak a complacent monopolist. It was unwilling to let go a business which was bringing in such a high margin. Fuji saw its strength was specialty chemicals, especially collagen used in photographic films. Fuji decided to move its investments into a line of cosmetics where collagen, due to its antioxidant properties, is used to rejuvenate the skin. Fuji further invested $4 billion to develop its expertise in creating an optical film for LCD flat-panel screens. In one market, of a thin sheet of WV (wide-view) film which is used to expand the LCD screen viewing angle in TVs, Fujifilm was the inventor and today enjoys a 100 per cent market share.

Kodak continued its development into digital cameras but its business model of selling cheap conventional cameras and make money on films could not work here. Besides, the introduction of mobile phones with cameras killed its new business.

On the contrary, Fuji's transition was very painful. It shed away superfluous distributors, the development labs, most managers and researchers while spending over $9 billion in acquiring companies. It was a stark choice; either reconstruct the business or die. All this in a country where the corporate culture does not allow companies to act fast, go on an acquisition spree or make deep cuts. It is a study in contrast that while Kodak acted like a typical inflexible Japanese firm, Fujifilm acted like an agile American one. Fujifilm had the foresight to dump the business when the margin was 60 per cent which Kodak was unwilling to do. Today, PepsiCo is undertaking a similar exercise to shift business to healthy food and beverages such as oatmeal and fruit juices.

Adapting your business to the changing external environment is required on a sustainable basis to remain relevant. We see some of these shifts already. Today's five largest global companies are Apple, Alphabet (Google), Microsoft, Amazon and Facebook. Ten years back, the big five were PetroChina, ExxonMobil, GE, China Mobile and Bank of China. Sometimes a decade is a lifetime!

Satya Nadella recently said that

Microsoft faces existential threat every 5 years, still, we're here. That means we are doing something right to stay at that level, to continue to question status quo. Our job is to meet the unmet, unarticulated needs of customers. That's where innovation comes from. I am not an expert on all the challenges but any digital system of identity that can help in solving or bringing down transaction cost or improve it—whether it is bank credit or help outcomes— is welcome. [2]

The first item to learn in an enterprise is to visualize the shape the shifting sands are taking due to an onslaught of winds of change. Learning to develop foresight is the key skill a company needs to survive and prosper in the VUCA future. The future comes slowly. Even for Kodak, there was more than a decade for it to change direction. Forty years back, Alvin Toffler predicted changes which will shape our society and businesses in his book *Future Shock*. He was not an oracle but someone who was looking at the emergence of early and weak signals which will have a profound effect in the future. Future seems to come suddenly only because we had not been looking for weak signals emanating from the environment. We must develop the ability in our organizations to look at long-term future a decade or more and prepare for it. The long-term future is generally stable, unlike short-term future, which can be from one to three years, where most uncertainty happens.

In a recent study tracking the real-world impact of competitive upheaval, it has been found that the fear of disruption is exaggerated. Also, the companies facing disruption generally take longer to respond than they expect, and an effective response is available for them. When disruption does affect a company, it's frequently because the enterprise was already vulnerable in some fundamental way; moreover, many incumbent companies accelerate their decline through their efforts to forestall it [3].

For example, we know that electric vehicles (EV) will be a major mode of transport in the long-term future, that is, the contours of long-term future are clearly emerging as the technology and regulatory environment accelerate. These EV require fewer parts than a conventional fuel motor vehicle. According to a study done by IHS Markit, vehicle sales in four largest markets, including India, would decline by 30 per cent by 2040, and BCG predicted on 2 November 2017 that by 2040, 19 per cent of vehicles sold will be electrically driven [4].

India has the third largest casting and forging industry in the world and 50 per cent of the output goes to automotive industry, both within the country and exports. How should these companies respond? We know that the aerospace industry is expanding and by 2030, there may be more than a million unmanned flying machines and drones in the United States and Europe alone. In addition, wind turbine industry is expanding. Should one start thinking about entry to these sectors today? Any change will require not only acquisition or development of technology but also operational transformations, new factories with Industry 4.0 inputs, skilling and re-skilling of personnel and so on. Today, these companies have the time to think various alternative futures and respond to the writing on the wall. If companies fail to address the issue today, five years from now may be too late to respond.

Learning to Develop Foresight

We start by first exploring how we think about the future, looking at ambiguity and uncertainty. Business leaders have, in the past, aligned their goals to a well-defined destination taking a well thought out path. In today's uncertain world where disruption can come from any direction, political, regulatory or technological, is it wise or even possible to define a single course and pursue it single-minded? How can you ensure the survival and sustainability of your business? In 1970, Alvin Toffler wrote *Future Shock*, cautioning us to the fast occurring changes in our environment and life, and suggested foresight as a key tool to deal with these changes. Future is not only stress and worry but also an opportunity and it requires a different set of tools and skills to navigate it which can be learnt.

According to Tricia Lustig, the author of *Strategic Foresight*, 'too much focus on the past leads to feelings of helplessness…. If you focus on potential, possible futures, and what you might learn from them, you rekindle your sense of wonder and love of possibility; you uncover energy for change' [5]. Since we cannot forecast the future and the future can evolve in several directions, foresight provides a window to explore which possible scenarios are probable, and from that, we can draw a strategic perspective as to what we can best influence.

It's a case of keeping your eyes peeled for early warning signs of emerging trends and as clarity emerges, visualize which of the various futures are likely to happen Do this right and you'll have yourself strategically positioned to influence, even co-create, the future you want—'unlike "ostrich" Blackberry, which completely overlooked the impact of the iPhone so that by the time the company realized what had happened, events had overtaken it' [6].

In an enterprise, a broad range of people, including representatives of all stakeholders, must put their minds together to visualize the range of options unfolding in future. The group should be multidisciplinary to include various perspectives, experience, education and competencies. According to Tricia Lustig, the future is a foreign country and culture shock is guaranteed. The future you see would have no relationship with the past and you need to, or be trained to, suppress your mindsets, biases and the baggage of their past experience. History is littered with organizations who did not see the future coming like IBM did not see the PC developed by Apple. Many large hotel companies still do not see that Airbnb is a threat to their business. If such companies with armies of strategic planners and deep research resources cannot see the future, is there any hope for the rest? Have you started thinking?

Developing foresight is not forecasting. You are not predicting the chances of an event happening but considering a range of futures, which can unfold in future, looking at 'weak signals' emanating today. Weak signals today might fade, or they might become the emerging trends but they will allow you to anticipate and adjust your plans or strategy as you go along rather than make big changes when future suddenly engulfs you. It can also let you spot opportunities, which your competitors are, as yet, unable to visualize. It is like discovering crevices, plugging them and choosing the most appropriate one that translate into a future opportunity, if not, leading to creation of disruptive ones.

The CEO or senior leaders should identify people with hidden, untapped intelligence within their organization, who read widely and actively participate in active professional networks. It is not too difficult to identify such persons through informal networks flourishing in the organizations, and CEO can bring groups of such people together and discuss the future in broader terms. Through such interaction, the CEO can weave one or more groups, which are multidisciplinary, and can bring a range of perspectives to the discussions. The CEO can then unleash this group intelligence by provoking their imagination and creativity, and leave them to identify and study 'weak signals' as they represent threats and opportunities for the business.

It is not too difficult to find such employees. They are the 'mavericks' and their reputation precedes their arrival. They are full of curiosity, they question everything and everybody, defy authority and generally their bosses are uncomfortable with them. At the same time, they respect and work with those who bring new knowledge and perspectives, and who can challenge them intellectually, they are patient with new colleagues and are good teachers. They take risks which others shun. Their DNA is already attuned to the seven skills and these are the people who are harbingers of change. Such persons should be nurtured by the CEOs to be their 'listening posts'.

Colonel T. E. Lawrence of *Lawrence of Arabia* fame was one such maverick. With an irregular force of Bedouin, he conquered the Fort of Aqaba, which everybody said was impossible. His confidential dossier read 'undisciplined', 'unpunctual' and 'untidy'. Once his commanding general warned him, 'I do not propose to let an overweening, crass lieutenant thumb his nose at his commander and get away with it' [7].

One interesting way is in setting up such groups and hunt for 'foxes' within the organization. Psychologist Philip Tetlock in his book *Expert Political Judgment* has demonstrated to a little surprise that the forecasters are usually not good. Even more surprisingly are his identification on the characteristics of good and bad forecasters.

Tetlock employs a distinction credited to the Greek poet Archilochus, but popularized by the philosopher Isaiah Berlin between hedgehogs and foxes. It is said that hedgehogs know one big thing and that they have an all-encompassing view of the world. They discover facts that confirm in what they already know is true. They rarely change their mind. Most experts fall into hedgehog category. Foxes know many little things; they are eclectic in their sources of information and nuanced in their judgements. Hedgehogs command more public attention but foxes make better forecasters. At the same time, foxes are diligent in pursuit of sources of information and are ready in revising their predictions with every new data becoming available [8].

As we have discussed in Chapter 8, the seven skills for the future, especially critical thinking, collaboration, etc., develop fast when such groups are allowed to flourish. Further, the group can interact with other internal and external experts, vendors, customers, front-end employees, etc., to widen their horizon and bring depth to the discussions. They should be provided with resources such as time, library, travel, etc., to facilitate their work which could be in addition to their regular responsibilities. As they begin to learn and gel together, their contribution to the organization through developing insights would increase.

The following model developed by us is an attempt to show the various learning flows within the organization, which is anticipating and responding to external change.

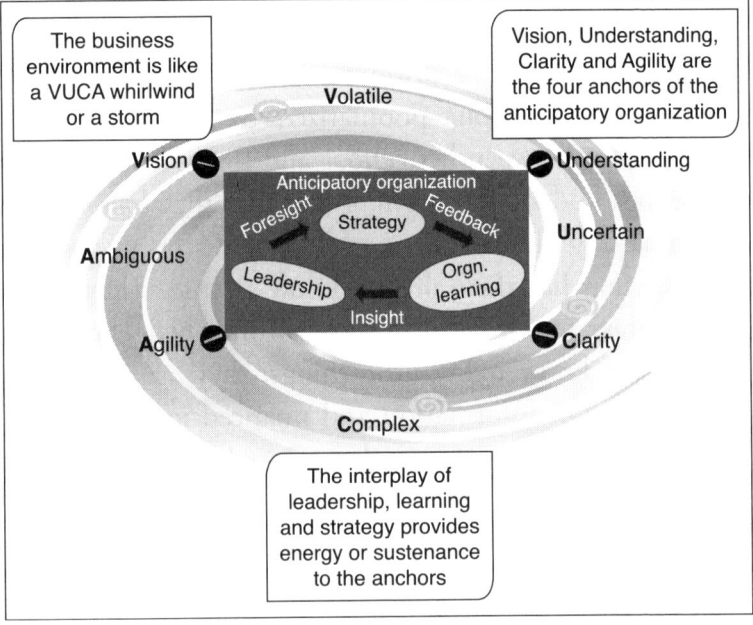

VUCA—Anticipatory Model©
Source: Authors' own.

VUCA represents the dynamic business environment in which the organization is anchored by the VUCA prime four interventions as described by Professor Bob Johansen [9] to amplify or dampen the effects of VUCA. These act as anchors which bring stability to the organization in times of great change. People within the organization identify 'early or weak signals' which have the possibility to threaten the organization or provide an opportunity for growth. These forces are studied by groups within the organization and insights presented to the management.

Volatile versus vision—Foresight exercise forces us to align our vision with the desired results and provide guideposts to reach there.

Uncertainty versus understanding—Invest in information gathering, interpretation and sharing. Look for facts, wherever possible, through data analytics and other tools.

Complexity versus clarity—Identification and understanding 'weak signals' make it possible to make sense of the world around us.

Ambiguity versus agility—Experiment, prototype fast and fail fast to test strategies for the various futures envisioned.

The CEO and senior leaders debate the insights and with the help of foresight groups create various scenarios of the future and often provide feedback which further helps fine-tune the offerings.

Learning Critical and Strategic Thinking Skills

The CEOs and the senior leaders are no longer the sole fountains of knowledge in a VUCA organization. Relative ease of access to information means that knowledge is no longer the preserve of the hierarchical elite but is created collaboratively, largely at the periphery of organizations where people directly interact with customers. These could be a salesperson in vehicle or two-wheeler showroom, medical representatives visiting doctors, loan personnel who interact with farmers and so on.

Knowledge is also created where two or more disciplines collaborate, such as marketing and R&D, sales and production, etc. A doctor in an interaction with a medical representative may talk about a treatment being developed by a rival organization or suggest that the ingredients of two tablets which are generally given together could be combined into one tablet to aid patient compliance. Does the company have any means of transferring this knowledge from the medical representative to senior management or R&D? The chances are not.

As we have seen earlier in the iceberg of ignorance, these employees are the first to spot opportunities and threats for the organizations they work for. However, their knowledge is fragmented and to convert their bits and pieces of knowledge into insights, they need to talk to other people in the organization, especially those who come from different disciplines and provide different perspectives. Through such dialogues, the critical thinking capacity of employees is developed and they become capable of providing strategic insights, innovations and solutions to the leaders.

Introduction of Industry 4.0 and changes in business models has made the process for group learning and thus creating valuable knowledge more urgent. A closer interaction with customers, enabled by new processes, products and services introduced by Industry 4.0 allows the manufacturers in communicating with customers more directly. They are able to tailor their business models more effectively. Products as diverse as aircraft engines and software are being increasingly offered as services, often on a pay-as-you-use basis. Pathological laboratory suppliers and imaging manufacturers are billing hospitals not on the sale of chemicals and instruments but as a share of patient billing.

In a PwC study of Industry 4.0, there is a shortfall seen towards building an analytical capability. The processes of Industry 4.0 provide huge data detailing customer demands, value chain, etc. If one cannot interpret the data in boosting efficiency, grow closer to the partners in the supply chain and develop products and services which the customers demand, the efforts are wasted [10].

One way of fostering group learning in organizations is creating community of practice (COP).

Community of Practice

Learning is a social activity. The days of Edison and Marie Curie are long gone where one brilliant mind working alone created knowledge. Today, whether in the area of scientific discovery or farming, people need to often sit together, exchange information, create new knowledge and hone their competencies. A farmer needs to consult other farmers, often in a village meeting place commonly known as *chaupal*, to learn about new seeds, new farming methods, how to obtain a loan, buy or lease, or rent tractor and even the prevailing rate for loan approval. Even formal training must be supplemented by informal knowledge groups to embed training objectives.

COP is essentially a peer-driven, non-hierarchical learning group, a group of practitioners, who share similar challenges, interact regularly, learn from and with each other and improve their ability to address their challenges and push the boundaries of their field. Senior leaders can launch COPs through sponsorship, nurturing and support. As companies expand and become more complex, no matter what organizational structure is in place, people must work with each other across reporting lines. Learning accelerates in these situations as different people with different knowledge and perspectives join resources to solve problems and innovate.

For example, an FMCG company can create COPs in the following format:

Function ⬇	Community of Practice ➡			
Strategy	Rural Marketing	Packaging	Supply Chain	Competitive Landscape
Marketing				New Product Development
Sales				
R&D				
Finance				

Members of COPs are also connected to other individuals and groups through social networks within and outside the organization. There is increasing evidence that employees learn new and complex skills as a result of being active participants in peer groups. We can leverage digital technologies to enable and encourage social networking and interactive collaborative engagements which further promote learning. Even reading has become collaborative as we browse, scan and bring related material to the attention of our social group, and through continuous dialogue take us into new directions of thinking.

In a VUCA world, even attrition is an ally and can be used as a resource for learning as many employees leave to broaden their experience. Some companies actively run alumni programmes to keep track of their employees and welcome them to return to the fold.

Do you know the secondary skills and experience possessed by your workforce? You will be surprised to know how much the employees know beyond their immediate work responsibilities. They can speak different languages or can offer their wide experience in helping the organization while interacting with clients, suppliers or distributors. Why don't you conduct a skill audit on the talents within your organization and post it on your internal website or dashboard? Let colleagues know where they can go to find information and discover opportunities to collaborate. Organizations can facilitate learning in innumerable ways which will ultimately strengthen the top and bottom line in a long-term sustainable manner.

It is possible that some organizations can teach people on how to learn fast, but most do not have this capability. It is a strong statement, yet proven in practice. They need to hire people who have proven capability of learning fast and have mastered this skill. These are the agile learners. They need to hire people who are continuous learners and those who can assist others in learning continuously. This is not an anecdote or a simple statement like attending a training programme. You always want people receptive to increasing their knowledge and engaged in developing new skills with added competencies and growth. For this to happen, organizations must look at new tools of recruitment that identify such wide attributes in advance.

One surprising attribute which is not related to a learning agility is intelligence, a demonstration of which was given by the inmates of a New York maximum security prison when their team defeated the Harvard University debating team, the national champions in 2015, at a debating event [11].

The Seven Principles of Learning

The following seven principles of learning (Institute of Research on Learning promoted by Xerox) provide the framework for creating a learning environment for an organization [12].

1. Learning is a definitely a social activity and not an individual activity. The social dynamics of relationships within an organization allow work to be

accomplished. Therefore, learning is faster in an organization that ensures the strengthening of the social fabric, especially related to peer relationship.

2. Knowledge, activity and social relations are closely intertwined. A group of knowledgeable persons would definitely have far greater knowledge collectively as compared to the most experienced individual experts. Strengthening peer and cross-functional groups allow people to learn from each other.

3. Learning is an act of membership. It is not just the activity of an individual but primarily a vehicle for continuous engagement with others. Senior management is especially prone to learning disabilities, a hard fact, with their increasing isolation at the top.

4. Knowing is engagement in practice. Acquiring information during training sessions without a clear road map for bringing the acquired learning into the workplace dissipates rapidly. It is only in the workplace where one can test knowledge and mindsets.

5. Engagement is inseparable from empowerment. Empowered employees can definitely take charge of their learning applying these at the workplace.

6. Failure to learn is the normal result of exclusion from participation. Greater is the number of employees participating in group or team activities, more will be the benefits to the organization from its learning.

7. We already have a society of lifelong learners, but what is learnt is not necessarily what organizations want. Realignment of personal and organizational learning objectives would therefore be a win-win situation.

The emphasis on this new learning process is on the worker's employability as compared to the job security.

Employees learn their work though conversation, collaboration and on-the-job experience. Enlightened corporations trust their people to pull in the resources they need. They've turned corporate learning upside down by putting the learners responsible for defining the curriculum. These corporations concentrate on building self-sustaining learning ecosystems.

However, even a good thing taken too far can be detrimental and so is with collaboration. Too much collaboration, overflowing e-mails and endless meetings can drain away employees' time and energy, and organizations should be alert to damaging effects of 'over collaboration'. At the organizational level, companies need to be more effective than collecting people from different departments into a room (real or virtual) and expect them to evince with greater ideas and outputs. This is an age-old practice. For example, value is added by individuals who are able to 'translate' across functional areas and help in bridging the potential silos. Firms can develop these individuals by creating 'rotations', through which entry-level employees can spend time with different departments, understand on various kinds of work requirements and also towards building networks [13].

A leader's job is to create a culture (see paragraph on Pixar in Chapter 2) that allows knowledge workers to learn—from their own experience, from each other and from customers, suppliers and business partners. The chief management tool that makes that learning happen is conversation.

One of the secrets of Zara's success is its ability to learn from customers. The brand trains and empowers its store employees and the managers to be particularly sensitive towards customer needs and wants. It empowers its sales associates and store managers to be at the forefront of customer research. They are told to carefully listen and capture customer comments, ideas for cuts, fabrics and keenly observe new styles that its customers are wearing. Such design ideas have the potential for being converted into unique Zara styles. Zara knows very well that the quicker it can respond, the more likely it is to succeed in supplying the right fashion merchandise at the right time across its global retail chain.

There have been instances where Zara has been able to bring particular products to its more than 7,000 stores worldwide within a week of those products being asked by customers, while many traditional competitors may take months to do the same turnaround [14].

The Industrial Age, with its neatly divided line and staff structure, is over and it's not coming back. The new organization structure, such as matrix organization, is a work in progress in a VUCA world and we still do not know what shape it will take. Meanwhile, social networking is flourishing and it is through these linkages that real learning and real work get done. Give employees the tools they need to create, communicate and collaborate, and create a safe, respectful work environment. Together they will creatively solve problems. Empowerment isn't optional today.

References

1. *The Economist.* 2012, 14 January. The Last Kodak Moment? Available at http://www.economist.com/node/21542796 (accessed 8 February 2018).
2. Choudhury, Karan. 2017, 8 November. Microsoft Faces Existential Threat Every 5 Yrs, Still We're Here: Nadella. *Business Standard.* Available at http://www.business-standard.com/article/companies/microsoft-faces-existential-threat-every-5-yrs-still-we-re-here-nadella-117110701601_1.html (accessed 8 February 2018).
3. Leinwand, Paul and Cesare Mainardi 2017, 27 September. The Fear of Disruption Can Be More Damaging Than Actual Disruption. *Strategy+Business.* Available at https://www.strategy-business.com/article/The-Fear-of-Disruption-Can-Be-More-Damaging-than-Actual-Disruption?gko=b4a17 (accessed 9 February 2018).
4. Lienert, Paul and Jessica Resnick-Ault. 2017, 14 November. Global Vehicle Sales to Fall by 2040, But Oil Demand to Rise: Study Predicts. *Business Standard.* Available at https://in.reuters.com/article/autos-electric-ihs/global-vehicle-sales-to-fall-by-2040-but-oil-demand-to-rise-study-predicts-idINKBN1DE2H7 (accessed 9 February 2018).
5. Lustig, Tricia. 2015. *Strategic Foresight: Learning from the Future.* Charmouth, Dorset, UK: Triarchy Press.
6. Alexander, Liz. 2016. Take Control of Your Business Destiny. *BL Magazine.* Available at http://www.lasa-insight.com/blog/wp-content/uploads/2016/03/BLMagazine_strategicforesight.pdf (accessed 9 February 2018).
7. Drew's Script-O-Rama. *Lawrence of Arabia Script—Dialogue Transcript.* Available at http://www.script-o-rama.com/movie_scripts/l/lawrence-of-arabia-script-transcript.html (accessed 9 February 2018).

8. Kay, John. 2016, 5 January. Foxes Make Good Economic Forecasts but Hedgehogs Can be Helpful. *Financial Times.* Available at https://www.ft.com/content/7dc1d310-b2e3-11e5-b147-e5e5bba42e51 (accessed 9 February 2018).
9. Johansen, Bob. 2007. *Getting There Early.* Oakland: Berrett-Koehler.
10. Geissbauer, Reinhard, Jesper Vedsø and Stefan Schrauf. 2016, 9 May. A Strategist's Guide to Industry 4.0. *Strategy+ Business.* Available at http://www2.caict.ac.cn/zscp/qqzkgz/qqzkgz_zdzsq/201606/P020160627404456089240.pdf (accessed 9 February 2018).
11. Gambino, Lauren. 2015, 7 October. Harvard's Prestigious Debate Team Loses to New York Prison Inmates. *The Guardian.* Available at https://www.theguardian.com/education/2015/oct/07/harvards-prestigious-debate-team-loses-to-new-york-prison-inmates (accessed 9 February 2018).
12. Wikipedia. *Institute for Research on Learning.* Available at https://en.wikipedia.org/wiki/Institute_for_Research_on_Learning (accessed 9 February 2018).
13. The Wharton School of the University of Pennsylvania. 2017, 9 November. Too Much Togetherness? The Downside of Workplace Collaboration. *Knowledge@Wharton.* Available at http://knowledge.wharton.upenn.edu/article/much-togetherness-downside-workplace-collaboration/ (accessed 9 February 2018).
14. Roll, Martin. *The Secret of Zara's Success: A Culture of Customer Co-creation.* Available at https://martinroll.com/resources/articles/strategy/the-secret-of-zaras-success-a-culture-of-customer-co-creation/ (accessed 9 February 2018).

Chapter 10
The Road Less Travelled: Learning in Entrepreneurship

It always seems impossible until it's done.

—Nelson Mandela

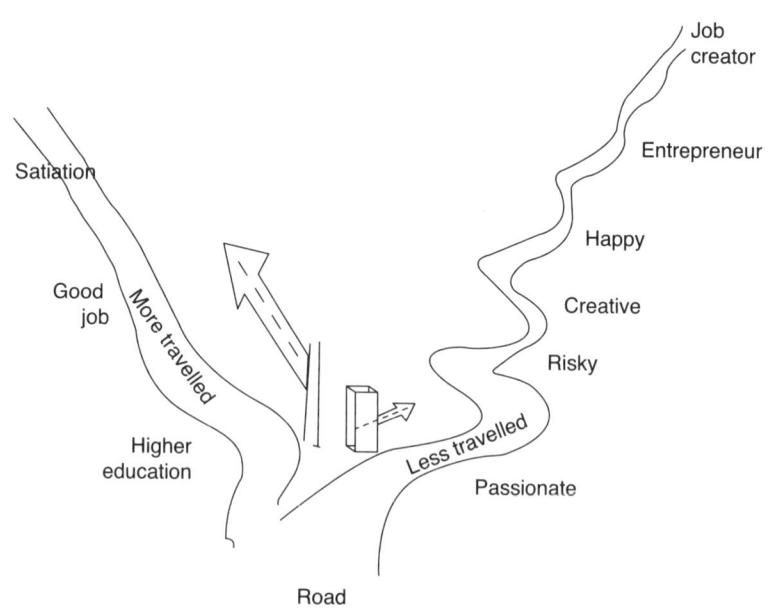

It is considered that obtaining higher degrees such as MBA from prestigious institutions can lead to good jobs and a decent earning throughout life. On the contrary, it is the entrepreneurs who as job creators turn out to be more successful, happier and driven by their passion to create something new. They add new value to old knowledge assets. This is exactly what these self-motivated so-called entrepreneurs do managing and mitigating risks while balancing their profession and life.

One such person is Kaushalendra from Patna, Bihar [1] (a state from northern part of India), who hailed from a very humble village family. His parents were teachers and that at an early age he was put to a school that was 50 km away from his native place, which provided free education. Being a meritorious and hardworking student, he got an entry into the prestigious Indian Institute of Technology and completed his bachelor of technology. During a short tenure in the job, straight out from the technical training, he was exposed to early learning. He could observe a visible gap between the living conditions in urban as compared to the rural areas and this economic divide triggered a purpose that he felt he could do something about. He later went on to acquire his master of business administration from Indian Institute of Management, Ahmedabad, yet another top and prestigious institution in its category. This fuelled his business acumen. Thus, driven by an innate desire, intrinsic motivation, passion and a fair risk-taking ability, he established Kaushalya Foundation in 2007, an agribusiness firm with brand Samriddhi [2]. With this entrepreneurial venture, he has been able to associate more than 20,000 farmers and 700 employees and successfully established a supply chain for frozen vegetables in one of the poorest parts of India.

Considering the aforementioned true story as one, though there are thousands, it is interesting to be curious as to what triggers entrepreneurship. While entrepreneurship is the process, it is the entrepreneur who is an individual engaged in setting up the enterprise. It is what researchers term as the power of reciprocal knowledge [3] while sharing and learning in their start-up journey. It is considered in the start-up journey that the entrepreneur acquires innovative capabilities and then translates them accordingly to suit the business. The same is true in start-up firms borne and emanating out of clusters such as Silicon Valley that promotes true level of entrepreneurship. It is imperative that there must exist a culture of knowledge within the start-up firm and its co-workers, who are ready to accept change, are adaptable and have the tenacity to accept challenges as an opportunity, rather than an impediment. Start-up firms may have a defined or an undefined system of communication exchange leading to knowledge transfer but what remains central to the discussion is if the culture embraces this process. In a fast-changing VUCA world, the challenges are extremely dynamic and thus mandate quick reception, decoding and response. The factor of timely agility is core to the learning and response, a therapy, which must be practised continuously by any start-up, its founders and co-workers. Perhaps, this is one major reason as to why some start-ups are more successful than others; it is their agility, precision and stealth woven around learning that they have mastered the timely response in a VUCA world.

Entrepreneurship is considered as a key element towards an economic growth of any nation. There are different growth rates existing amongst different cities. This may be as an outcome of a differentiated level of entrepreneurial activities and endowments towards entrepreneurship. Yet knowledge transfer is one of the key elements that assist in such entrepreneurial activities. What makes these individuals as entrepreneurs and places them above the rest is the risk-taking propensity towards the creation of new business. There are some studies indicating the outcome of economic growth around few geographical locations where entrepreneurship is centred around [4]. The socio-economic fabric of the cluster is threaded around this dimension of entrepreneurship and it impacts the economic activity and so does it accelerate the true level of entrepreneurship around the system. As a general learning around the world, it may be intermediately interpreted that there is a reciprocal relationship between the entrepreneur and the local culture (like the biggest diamond exporters from India come from Palanpur area of Gujarat), which intermediates as a catalyst and the environment that leverage this phenomenon for heightened economic activity. The bigger curiosity is what triggers this economic activity and subsequently what it results into. It is like the chicken and egg as to, which came first? Yet in entrepreneurship, the key process in establishing an enterprise, it is documented that the entrepreneur is the key driving factor. Environment, etc., may act as an accelerator to this entrepreneurship process. Thus, differential economic growth amongst the cities may be causality between the culture and individuals whom we term as an entrepreneur, who finally fosters economic growth.

Thus, an interesting point of discussion emanates as to why not have an entrepreneurship policy that stimulates economic growth and also becomes a necessary condition for employment generation and reducing poverty [5]. Policies can foster innovation, an essential in entrepreneurship and wealth creation. These can become intrinsic drivers in the entire process fostering what we term as opportunity-driven entrepreneurship. The fundamental ground level assistance even if it is miniature can gear the entire economic activity. The central focus remains around how the individual masters the art of exploiting the opportunities in creating an enterprise, which in turn creates a series of economic activities around it. However, studies complement and connect a positive relationship between the process, which is entrepreneurship and economic growth [6].

There are some entrepreneurial implications too. We understand that the prospective entrepreneurs approaching [7] venture capitalist towards funding their enterprise is solely depended upon the developed risk-taking ability and their refined or developed entrepreneurial orientations. Most successful stories are evidence that the first trance and tranche of capital follows the next if the first one is effectively used. There is no fixed solution or a predefined intended outcome that after every investment the result will be favourable. The core revolves around the entrepreneur, the learning ability he/she exhibits and the rapid modifications it can improvise in the entire entrepreneurship journey, which can be gruesome and killing if not followed judiciously. The entrepreneur apart from being an innovator must have dynamic skills of improving techniques assisting the deliverables. There is no platter, which can or will continuously leverage the performance. This implies that by having a great idea, followed by raising a requisite fund, having a great team followed by innate entrepreneurial desire with a solid passion and a reasonable dimension of characteristics may just be few triggers in the entrepreneurship process. But the success is not guaranteed in the journey of the entrepreneur in a VUCA world. The days are gone when the environment was less turbulent and could have been predicted. We are living in a dynamic VUCA world where the velocity of change is undefined, unexpected and unknown. Thus, can we predict the success rates of these entrepreneurs, entrepreneurship as their process and the enterprise as their outcome? Mostly, we shall say no!

There are umpteen challenges in measuring the readiness for entrepreneurship [8]. The factors that are established in this enterprise creation process range from self-efficacy, the locus of control, creativity, risk undertaking propensity, a capability to sense opportunity and translate it into a successful business model, leadership skills and other cognitive traits. Tenacity matters! Culture may support; the knowledge transfer mechanisms may exist yet the key to entrepreneurship in a VUCA world is the constant learning ability, improvisation methods, tenacity and resilience followed by the power of adaptability. Without this, it is virtually impossible to demonstrate success in the journey of enterprise creation. We term this as an essential ingredient in the entrepreneurial framework and in defining the personality of the entrepreneur. As entrepreneurship teachers, we understand the limitations that translating the aforementioned is not an easy task as it is very dynamic and revolves around a deeper understanding on sociology, psychology, technology management, learning ability and ability to translate knowledge. The world is rapid, and coexistence is a challenge. It changes with geography and along with the levels of complexity and its response. Can it be tailored? Not yet! There are no defined solutions.

In an interesting study, it was posited as to who lives longer? Start-ups or spin-offs? [9] Previous results have indicated that second-generation entrepreneurs with a surviving first generation had a better chance of survival. Spin-offs are a result of value creation by its seeding entrepreneur who may intend to venture in a new direction; it may be related or unrelated, but the dimensions required to stay ahead as an entrepreneur are more likely to be the same. But the truth is different in this VUCA world. The expertise required is very unique, with each dimension emerging to be as complex and unique. In today's turbulent nature of business environment, industry-specific knowledge and its differentials must be closely understood. This is where we term the nature of volatility. There is no straight line or even a predefined curve, which is predictable. The newer start-ups will have to create their own trajectory, which ultimately may or may not be unique but certainly will seek improvisations in the journey. We term this as improvised innovations with time in the differential world of VUCA. Each entrepreneur may thus have to engage, at times, in reinventing the wheel with improvised business models [10] for a long-term sustainability of the start-ups.

The theatre of start-ups, largely speaking, has changed drastically over the years. Previously, the world witnessed with localized or focused geographies emerging as start-up cities or nations. The world is different now. Clusters promoting entrepreneurship have emerged with each learning cycle in the journey of the true level of entrepreneurship by nations, wherein the culture promotes towards wealth creation. Though it is catching up in countries like India and other developing nations, the underline query remains the same as to what differentiates a successful nation from others in an economic process. Is it entrepreneurship? Certainly, it is. Yet the key lies in translating the existing knowledge both in success and failure by these start-ups. Developed nations have improvised on this learning, yet many of us remain silent and succumb to the dynamic world of VUCA. Have we learnt from some failures of start-ups?

Often, start-ups fail due to poor scaling-up strategy but they persist on moving on fast expansion in spite of many recorded failures. Narendra Murkumbi of Shree Renuka Sugars fame, considered to be a promising and leading entrepreneur, succumbed to his desire in speeding upscaling. Due to this, the sugar king of India piled up huge debts to expand his empire. As is inherent in a VUCA world, the future did not pan out as planned leading to large and unsustainable losses and he had to relinquish control over his business [11]. It was an inherent desire to grow too fast and too furious [12], as we have described in our previous book *The VUCA Company*, an obsession with fast expansion when consolidation was required. Murkumbi, with tremendous foresight, did initiate a revolutionary business model, never attempted before in India, that is, to import raw sugar from Brazil and refine it in India. This would balance out the uncertain demand-supply situation, which plagues the Indian sugar industry. To this end, he bought two sugar companies in Brazil with their own plantations in quick succession. When doing something new for the first time, prudence dictates that you first take baby steps, learn and then move forward. Perhaps, Murkumbi should have purchased one company and should have learned the new business model which included plantation management for which he had no prior experience before buying the second one. The rush inside the entrepreneur to stay ahead as a wealth multiplier, without understanding and absorbing the prevalent changes enforced by VUCA, led to the downfall of the empire.

Perhaps, an uncontrolled lust to grow, without keeping in mind the rules for stability, especially when the market is not fully explored, is a lethal combination of unexpected and unknown which leads to failure. Entrepreneurs usually fail to measure this critical dimension in their journey and with an inflated appetite to stay ahead of the competition, followed by the lust to grow exponentially. They do not fully appreciate the learning principle enunciated by Peter Senge, author of *The Fifth Discipline*. He says the paradox is that to do things faster, you have to go slower. It essentially means:

1. Check undisciplined speed of growth. Pause.
2. Reflect, make course correction, learn and embed learning in the organization.
3. Move forward.

Recently two start-up failures, Snapdeal in e-commerce space and Stayzilla, the homestay pioneer, which slipped on the fast expansion banana peel, reinforced the necessity of learning with reflection.

In the words of the founders of Snapdeal:

> We started growing the business much earlier than the right economic model and the market fit was actually figured out. It followed diversification, with new projects being initiated. We, however, did not realise that we still hadn't perfected the first or even made it profitable. The team we started building with added capabilities were actually for a much bigger size of business than what was actually required with the present scale… a large amount of capital with ambition can be a lethal potent mix driving a company to defocus from its core. We did realise what that happened to us but too late. Technically, speaking, we had started doing too many things, and all of us starting with myself and Rohit, are to blame for it. [12]

One of the reasons cited by the founders of Stayzilla for their downfall was lack of focus on cash flow, which led to draining of cash, a common cause for start-up failures.

All start-ups should remember the banker's motto: 'Topline is vanity, bottom line is sanity, cash flow is reality'. Time and again, history has shown that our addiction for top line growth blinds us from seeing the draining cash.

It also makes us vulnerable to a black swan-induced recession. It is no surprise that management guru Professor Ram Charan identifies cash as the topmost priority in his article 'Basics of Moneymaking'. He says that the key factors to making money are the same in any business: cash, margin, velocity, return and growth. These factors should be at the forefront of all analysis and decision-making in every job. It is understood that no business survives long without liquidity. It is important that one should know how much cash one's business generates and that how much cash it consumes. What are the sources of it? What drains it? What's the timing of the inflows and outflows, and how is it changing? More revenues (sales) often imply more cash. Yet we know that growing a business does consume cash. How fast can the company expand without straining its cash flow is question to ponder to [11].

Aspirations are good but overambitious can be disastrous, if the VUCA wave [13] is not understood properly. Entrepreneurs must polish their capabilities rather hone them with time. The business environment is not the same all the time, especially when the industry is different. To add to the list, if the entrepreneur is too ambitious and intends to magnify the existing growth by entering into too many industry verticals simultaneously, it may be catastrophic. Capabilities are defined for each and it takes years to master it, even if there is an intended inorganic growth. Successful firms stay put their bet on organic growth to a great extent and after measuring the risk, adventure as a calculated one. Remember, growth may be fast; keeping it steady is a daunting task, and downfall with one wrong move and interpretation may be imminent. Top line as vanity or bottom line as results, which one are preferred by these entrepreneurs? Course correction and regular improvisation are mandatory for the successful entrepreneur. It is said the curse of 'know-all' is the starting point of demise, even if the start-up model is sound.

A recent Indian study of 330 start-ups and 560 founders has shown that successful ventures are those where the founders have several years (a decade or more) of experience compared to those which die out. Experienced founders had deeper domain knowledge (the disciplined mind) and are better equipped to manage people and a wider network of investors and employees. They also have greater multidisciplinary knowledge picked up tacitly over the years (the seven skills). The short-lived start-ups are largely launched by young entrepreneurs who have the advantage of viewing the world from new perspective and therefore have great ideas. They fail in implementation due to poor grasp of various types of formal and tacit knowledge which go into a successful business [14].

We know from the natural world that systems—biological or social entities—which lack effective feedback loops do not survive. Slow adaptors fail in any evolutionary and competitive environment. This is also the case with man-made organizations. The fall of Lehman Brothers, General Motors and Kodak have only underlined this principle.

This is primarily due to dysfunctional learning of the promoters with a poor understanding of the complex, uncertain and chaotic business ecology termed as VUCA (volatility, uncertainty, complexity and ambiguity). Our mechanical clockwork model is behind these organizations' assumption that future is calculable, plan-able, predictable and engineer-able. The reality is that the world is a complex ecosystem where future is unpredictable and chaotic. Strategic planning assumes one can predict the outcome and control the process. When there is ambiguity and uncertainty, there is no ability to predict and control. This is the business environment we are facing now [11].

References

1. Bannerjee, Debopam. 2017, 24 August. *IIM Topper Making Crores By Selling Vegetables, Transformed 20,000 Farmers' Life.* Available at https://www.kenfolios.com/iim-topper-making-crores-selling-vegetables-transformed-20000-farmers-life/ (accessed 9 February 2018).
2. Fragrance of Success. *Why is this Gold Medalist from IIM (A) Selling Vegetables?* Available at https://fragranceofsuccess.wordpress.com/2016/01/15/why-is-this-gold-medalist-from-iim-a-selling-vegetables/ (accessed 9 February 2018).
3. Morrison, Alison. 2000. 'Entrepreneurship: What Triggers It?' *International Journal of Entrepreneurial Behavior & Research* 6 (2): 59–71.
4. Rahman, Mizan and Nafeez Fatima. 2011. 'Entrepreneurship and Urban Growth: Dimensions and Empirical Models'. *Journal of Small Business and Enterprise Development* 18 (3): 608–626.
5. Edoho, Felix Moses. 2016. 'Entrepreneurship Paradigm in the New Millennium: A Critique of Public Policy on Entrepreneurship'. *Journal of Entrepreneurship in Emerging Economies* 8 (2): 279–294.

6. Hafer, R. W. 2013. 'Entrepreneurship and State Economic Growth'. *Journal of Entrepreneurship and Public Policy*, 2 (1): 67–79.

7. Kropp, Fredric, Noel J. Lindsay and Aviv Shoham. 2008. 'Entrepreneurial Orientation and International Entrepreneurial Business Venture Startup'. *International Journal of Entrepreneurial Behavior & Research*, 14 (2): 102–117.

8. Ruiz, Jesús, Domingo Ribeiro Soriano and Alicia Coduras. 2016. 'Challenges in Measuring Readiness for Entrepreneurship'. *Management Decision* 54 (5): 1022–1046.

9. Furlan, Andrea. 2016. 'Who Lives Longer? Startups vs Spinoffs Founded as Proprietorships'. *International Journal of Entrepreneurial Behavior & Research* 22 (3): 416–435.

10. Ghezzi, Antonio. 2017. 'Reinventing the Wheel as an Emerging Business Model Innovation Paradigm'. *Strategic Direction* 33 (5): 1–4.

11. Joshi, M. and S. Abidi. 2017, October. 'Too Fast Too Furious'. *Indian Management*. Available at https:// poseidon01.ssrn.com/delivery.php?ID=0800240920240 99096117101099121094110032078062093055026025 12700211211406607002009711309801805801502003 80531180080960820650911020540750210790310791 03066119088069026052008016027088080082096070 06612009509202000100112107109506408401007007 2123126112000116&EXT=pdf (accessed 9 February 2018).

12. Rukhaiyar, Ashish. 2017, 22 February. Snapdeal Lays off Staff, Founders to Forgo Pay. *The Hindu*. Available at http://www.thehindu.com/business/Industry/snapdeal-founders-take-100-pay-cut-admit-errors-in-strategy/article17347080.ece (accessed 9 February 2018).

13. Chauhan, A., M. Joshi and S. Abidi. 2017, November. 'Riding the VUCA Wave'. *Indian Management.* Available at https://www.magzter.com/article/Business/Indian-Management/Riding-The-VUCA-Wave (accessed 9 February 2018).
14. Chitnis, Shailesh. 2011, 11 January. The Secret Sauce Behind a Successful Indian Start-up. *LiveMint.* Available at http://www.livemint.com/Companies/gIzjSNuByko PFmPIVopk5J/The-secret-sauce-behind-a-successful-Indian-startup.html (accessed 9 February 2018).

Chapter 11
Future-ready

You can't stop the waves, but you can learn how to surf.

—Jon Kabat-Zinn

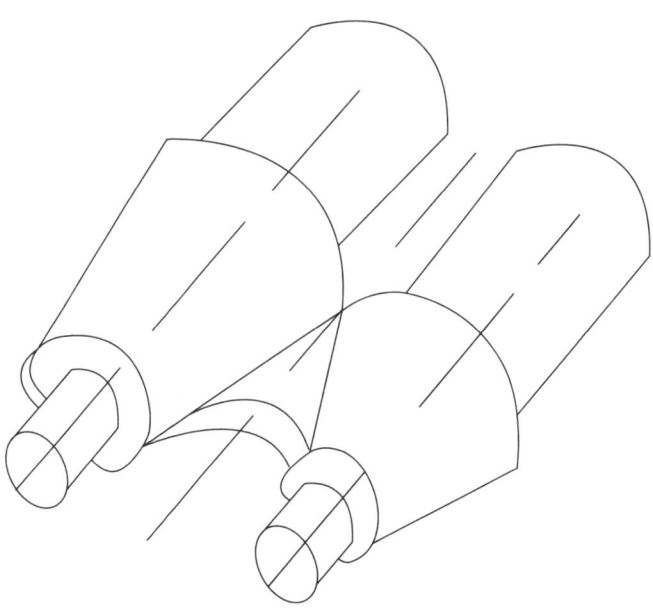

Future Ready

Every day, we see a new job description, a new career emerging, for example, learning engineer, chief data officer (CDO), chief listening officer (CLO), even cyborg anthropologist (the study of man–machine interface) and so on. An individual joining today can expect to change jobs six to seven times over the course of working life, and four of these jobs don't exist yet. Future readiness is the capacity to anticipate trends in emerging technology and in the wider business environment, including social trends which impact your company and the industry. Future does not come suddenly. Weak signals herald its arrival. Education, which is slow to change and is generally obsolete by the time you graduate, cannot prepare you to be ready when opportunity knocks. How many of us have the signal receptive ability, leave aside translating it? Yet some have both and are star achievers in today's and future context. But, in general, it is observed that most of us are complacent and star performers in our own comfort zones! The reality is different in a highly turbulent and vortex-filled VUCA world.

The New Age professionals are currently living in a time of unprecedented changes followed by disruption. We can certainly predict for them that the working environment will accelerate its uncertainty and unpredictability. The complexity level is increasing exponentially. Thus, a growth mindset and constantly evolving sets of skills are required to stay ahead in the turbulent business environments.

To give an example, Tesla Motors launched a new industry in itself that is EV which are shaking the contours of the traditional vehicle industry. While the EV market is still at a relatively early stage of development, it is poised to reshape industries and communities the world over. Today, the streets of every town in India is cluttered with e-rickshaws, and different types of vehicles will soon be seen on the road. Production of EV, EV components and EV infrastructure such as maintenance workshops and charging stations would create many types of new jobs, which do not exist today. For the first time, renewal energy costs are lower than coal. These are some of the examples of the green shoots of future businesses and which may develop into global trends and create jobs for the future.

When we watch the arrival of new technologies like AI, Blockchain and machine learning, we think of job losses. They're definitely going to cause a lot of jobs to disappear, but they're also going to create a large number of new jobs. Either way you look, the future is a killer of status quo. Are you prepared?

Besides technology, green shoots appear in many other industries such as leisure industry 'dogs on rent' is one such example of creating a business of providing dogs as jogging companions or another company which provides clothes for children (who grow out of clothes very fast) on monthly rent. Entrepreneurs observe early trends in emerging needs and convert these into business opportunities. Each trend offers multiple opportunities for employment. Change often begins with individual cases and social media may amplify it. Look for weak signals today, which may turn into major industries tomorrow. Start observing and be a great thinker, what you see flourishing today shall be obsolete and so shall be you, unless newer strategic and stealth skill sets are acquired on the journey.

The world is changing fast and that we need to become a society of people constantly engaged in learning new things, says Julie Friedman Steele, chairman of the Board of the World Future Society. At the same time, we are also going to need a strategic shift towards our learning process. The question is how do we learn? With so many rapid advances quickly, it shall be difficult and challenging for teachers and trainers to keep abreast with the latest thinking. Therefore, technology will come handy in finding the best sources of information to keep our knowledge and skills current [1].

It is seen that majorly people have an obsession with acquiring and flashing degrees. The future does not belong to those who boast about their school and past accomplishments. Today, a career can be considered a series of episodes where one job may not have much in common with what you did earlier. First came blue-collar (factory worker) followed by the white-collar (office worker). Now is the time for 'any collar'. This term coined by IBM is about skills, not degrees. If you have the right skills, there's a career waiting for you at IBM. For example, specific to Blockchain, IBM has a new programme that offers Blockchain digital badges for certification, the graduates which are able to display their certified skills on their resumes or LinkedIn profiles. Flashing acquired degrees may become redundant but not those you create yourself. The old order knowledge may seep in some high degree of complacency, as mentioned earlier and can be devastating.

Individuals, with the right potent and curiosity to learn, who acquire appropriate skill sets will be clear winners.

Vanitha Narayanan, chairperson of IBM India, says that a major reason for the programme is that college is not affordable for a lot of kids. 'And even when they graduate college with an undergraduate degree, many of them do not have the necessary skills', she said [2].

There is no clear correlation between higher education and a great entrepreneur/innovator or a successful professional career. If this causality existed, we would not have witnessed the likes of Facebook Founder Mark Zuckerberg who is a college dropout. Fifteen per cent of Google staff has no college degree. Our education system was designed to produce mass production workers for factories in the Industrial Age and we don't expect it to change in the foreseeable future. Today, we live in an age where knowledge is increasingly replacing capital as the currency of the economy. From mass manufacturing, we are entering the age of mass customization. Peter Diamandis, who was named one of 'the World's 50 Greatest Leaders' by *Fortune Magazine* in 2014, had said that between 2016 and 2022, there would be as many technological developments taking place as between 1900 and 2000.

According to Satya Nadella, CEO of Microsoft:

> [W]hile you may believe you're an expert in a particular field, it's always a bad idea to assume you've reached your full potential and can rest on your laurels. Aside from it being hard enough to assimilate every single aspect of a job type, the constant progression of technology and culture changes the rules along the way as well. One of

them is a 'know-it-all' and the other is a 'learn-it-all'. Indeed, the 'learn-it-all' shall always achieve better than the other one even if the 'know-it-all' kid starts with a much more innate capability. If that applies to boys and girls at school, I think it also applies to CEOs like me, and entire organizations, like Microsoft. [3]

He further advises that it's better to stay on one's toes, never assuming that learning is complete. Failures are definitely not bad if they come as a learning opportunity. Nadella is building this kind of learning culture at Microsoft [3].

If you think of life as a school, learning is open and continuous. It must come from our surroundings, provided one matures and is receptive to newer dimensions. This knowledge can emanate from anyone around, irrespective of gender, age, culture, religion, geography, etc. There must be humility to accept yes, I don't know this and that there is a willingness to acquire this newer knowledge and move ahead and thus confidently facing challenges.

Some people say that they will not accept a job with less salary than they are getting today or others say they will not move out of their city for better careers or not move out of their chosen line of career. Today, everyone with whatever qualification or experience, or position can expect disruption in their career. Those who put many conditions in pursuing their career opportunities take risk of not having a career at all as every day of unemployment can decrease their skill set and make it more difficult to find jobs at all. A job can get you a better job as you continue to hone your skills. At some extremities, one can create newer opportunities within the existing profile and, as an entrepreneurial learner, stay ahead of others. For this to happen, one will have to have a foresight, as a strategic advantage in understanding future skills or competencies required.

The future belongs to those with humility, integrity and authenticity. The work in future will be performed by project teams, and ability to perform in a team would matter more than being a 'star performer'. You can be the architect of the future or its victim. The choice is yours.

Take time off regularly to think where you intend to be in your career, then manoeuvring backward, creating action plans with a specific, defined steps and milestones can motivate you in getting up the ladder. This is called a reverse integrated learning mechanics and must be continuous.

Begin executing it. You can definitely course correct your strategy based on the results of your continuous efforts. Thus, when the opportunity presents itself, push or nudge yourself to learn, grow and expand your comfort horizons simultaneously. If you're still not comfortable taking a giant leap in new strategic directions, do take smaller ones initially, until you are prepared and confident in making a more radical shift in career focus or priorities. Sitting around and repeating the same kind of work may be catastrophic. Actively seek newer ways to learn, add new skills and gain hands-on experience in areas that are unfamiliar. Start exercising your problem-solving abilities in a new and novel way.

Volunteer for assignments which others think are too difficult or too risky. One of the Indian actors from Bollywood Saif Ali Khan refused the lead role, which was taken as an opportunity and executed by Shah Rukh Khan in the big box office hit movie *Dilwale Dulhaniya Le Jayenge*. Shah Rukh Khan did many career-risky, negative or unglamorous roles, in spite of being a top star, such as *Darr*, *Baazigar* or *Chak De! India*. In every role, he honed his acting skill. There is no doubt in anyone's mind where Shah Rukh Khan is today. Thus, accepting newer challenges, acquiring and honing them with time is the need for today.

New Skills Are Always Learned on the Job

Purposefully, you must put yourself in situations which are challenging, such as volunteering to work on projects demanding to try newer things. This may engage working with a new set of people or teaming up with colleagues in experimenting with better and creative ideas. To get different results, one will have to try different things. In order to get better ones, you must keep trying more and more things. In such situations, learning will be continuous while adjusting to achieve better with each new effort as one steers in the journey.

In many companies, CSR is throwing up new avenues not only to test your skills in a new environment but also to bring the satisfaction that you are contributing to the society. Volunteering for hard or unpleasant tasks such as CSR work in rural areas where living conditions will be less comfortable than what you are used to will make you stand out from your competition. Fewer rivals mean less competition. This may follow with an increase in valuable rewards for those pushing through their limits and accomplishing these challenging tasks. Learning continuously and improvising makes us all more versatile, more resilient and more successful at solving newer problems. The confidence you gain will propel you to start applying focused effort on accomplishing larger goals. Brainstorming newer solutions and by shunning away complacency, you will emerge as a renewed and effective innovator.

Career audit or career SWOT analysis is the foundation which allows you to view your strengths and weaknesses in a more realistic light over which you can lay the plans for building a career enhancement or career change. SWOT cannot take place unless you learn to be brutally honest with your self-assessment. Generally, we overestimate our strengths and underestimate weaknesses and we also overestimate our ability to bring change and underestimate the attitude and effort required to do the same. Discussion with people who care about you and whom you trust can help you get a realistic assessment of your strengths and weaknesses. They can help you gauge your skills and pinpoint your true calling.

Business leaders know that any challenge can (and should) be a learning event. Lifelong learning is what helps us ultimately reach our full potential. As managers of people in today's knowledge worker economy, leaders should realize that fostering employee learning is critical to bring about sustainable growth. Leadership should create a culture for tolerance of failure and can even go one step further by encouraging early failures as an opportunity to learn. Growth is not possible without challenging yourself. One step backward can lead to two steps forward.

Welcome to the newly defined Social Age. We humans can be truly identified as social, down to the very core. This implies that social is not just in what we do but it is what we are! We keep connecting, communicating, sharing our ideas, etc., and at times warnings too! Conversation is the source of knowledge today. Innovation is done in groups. Any opportunity for people to come together and introduce to new and diverse people and groups will foster discovery and innovation like nothing else.

Till a few years back, connectivity was limited to villages and nearby towns, largely face-to-face between people. Today, 2 billion humans are connected worldwide with only one or two degrees of separation, and the connectivity is increasing exponentially. People coming online on the web every day are increasing. The world is getting smarter with smartphones. Very soon, most of us will be just a thumb press away with others [4].

Not only the humans are social animals, they are also thinking animals. This is especially important to the millennials, especially if your company wants to be innovative and at the forefront of your industry. Millennials bring a fresh perspective and embrace technology as fish. Modify your learning programme to strike a balance between employee satisfaction and performance yardsticks. In the Social Age, millennials take empowerment for granted and need to believe in the vision, but they still look for support. In the current industrial age, leaders are focused on 'buy-in'. This is largely through manipulative motivation. However, in the Social Age, employees, once they see the objective, empower themselves. Wise leaders delight in this; they give up their role as controllers; they become facilitators and motivators.

In VUCA, your growth trajectory is unlikely to be a continuous one, like climbing a ladder. Rather it shall be more like scaling a mountain, passing through both crests and troughs. The ability to learn continuously and adapting will allow you to survive the terrain comprising of undefined troughs and then assist in seizing opportunity during moments of the crest. Resilience and adaptability are skills that should be in everyone's kitty. These skills will come handy by deploying the power of reflection revisiting your experience and identifying what really went wrong and how you can rectify in future.

Each morning, get up and tell yourself that you will do something new today. Every night, before going to bed, reflect on the day's events and try to uncover the insight into your behaviour and, thus armed with this knowledge, seek change.

VUCA presents an unusual opportunity to rise and shine. The only way to seize it is through self-education and self-learning.

Learn from the honeybee. Identify the right flower but for this, one may have to go against the wind more than with it, pick the nectar and move ahead. Learn from the disciplined ants that bring order to chaos. They move in a defined line while progressing in teams, sharing and transferring knowledge candidly to each fellow ant, providing a smooth passage rather than an obstruction on progress. Learning is continuous; it never ends. Learning starts from the past, applied in present and envisioned in a context for tomorrow. The art of sensing and staying ahead for a learner is must, as we must remember the world is very punishing to those who are unable to adapt and respond to in a VUCA world.

Start learning today. No! Start learning 'now'.

References

1. Moran, Gwen. 2016, March. These Will Be the Top Jobs in 2025 (And the Skills You'll Need to Get Them). *Fast Company*. Available at https://www.fastcompany.com/3058422/these-will-be-the-top-jobs-in-2025-and-the-skills-youll-need-to-get-them (accessed 9 February 2018).

2. Johni, Sujit. 2017, 28 June. IBM India Plans to Launch 12+2 Programme for New Collar Jobs. *The Times of India*. Available at https://timesofindia.indiatimes.com/business/india-business/ibm-india-plans-to-launch-122-programme-for-new-collar-jobs/articleshow/59354167.cms (accessed 9 February 2018).

3. D'Mello, Gwyn. 2017, 26 April. *Satya Nadella Has Just One Piece of Brilliant Advice for People Who Want to Succeed at Their Work*. Available at https://www.indiatimes.com/technology/news/satya-nadella-has-just-one-piece-of-brilliant-advice-for-people-who-want-to-succeed-at-their-work-276445.html (accessed 9 February 2018).

4. Babbit, Mark and Ted Coine. 2014. *A World Gone Social: How Companies Must Adapt to Survive*. Nashville, Tennessee: AMACOM.

Annexure: Personal SWOT Analysis

One of the hardest things to do alone is to effectively carry out a skills self-evaluation before setting up clear objectives in a PLP.

Knowing where one is at a given time is not an easy task due to a variety of reasons, one being the difficulty in being objective with oneself, the ability to take a step back and see things as they are, without being overshadowed by emotive aspects.

A SWOT analysis can really help in gaining clarity and setting realistic objectives and is a simple tool that can be used alone, but which can be further exploited with the help of a coach.

The idea is to start out by looking at where you are now in terms of your goals, aims and objectives, and to discover where effort needs to be put in order to reach your goals.

Personal SWOT Analysis Exercise			
Please circle the box you wish to select			
	Yes	**No**	**Score**
A. Strength			
Have you updated your CV during the past six months?	1	0	
Do you possess unique skills/ competencies your colleagues do not have?	1	0	
Do you have any outstanding skills/ competencies for which you are called upon often for assignments?	1	0	
Do your friends/family/colleagues see any outstanding skills/competencies in you?	1	0	
Have you been part of any multifunctional team in past one year?	1	0	
Have you attended any training programme in past one year which can help your next promotion?	1	0	
Have you attended any national/ international conference in past one year?	1	0	
Have you been offered a lateral movement position in your organization in past one year?	1	0	
Have you read any professional/self-development book in past one month?	1	0	
Have you read any professional/self-development magazine in past one week?	1	0	

B. Weakness	Yes	No	Score
Do you lack experience which would prevent your next promotion?	0	1	
Have you been passed over for any promotion in past one year?	0	1	
Are there family/geographical/time/financial constraints in seeking higher roles?	0	1	
Have you sought negative feedback from your mentors/colleagues/friends/family?	1	0	
Can any weakness in personality/character derail your career (e.g., procrastination/low self-esteem)?	0	1	
Do you have a plan for overcoming your weaknesses/negative traits?	1	0	
Have you tried and failed at any venture?	1	0	
Have you discussed above with your mentor/colleagues/friends/family?	1	0	
Have you taken steps to avoid such failures?	1	0	
Do you have a plan if you are suddenly offered a VRS today?	1	0	
C. Opportunities	**Yes**	**No**	**Score**
Are you a member of any professional social group such as those on LinkedIn?	1	0	
Have you messaged in your online social group within past one week?	1	0	
Is your industry growing in present recession?	1	0	

(continued)

(continued)

Have there been requests from other divisions/departments than your own to join new assignment/team in past one year?	1	0
Do you talk to 'nots' in your industry (not your customer/supplier/employee)?	1	0
Do you bring significant 'nots' insights to your management?	1	0
Have you brought any competitors' weaknesses/strengths to the attention of your management in past one year?	1	0
Do you have a systematic process of scanning opportunities in your industry?	1	0
Have you looked at opportunities in areas other than your current function in same company/same industry/different industry in past one year?	1	0
Do you have strong referrals in your company/industry/other industries to refer you to potential job opportunities?	1	0
D. Threats	**Yes**	**No**	**Score**
Do you have a list of possible threats to your company/industry in next three years?	1	0
Does changing technology threaten your job?	0	1
Is there strong competition for your next promotion?	0	1
Do your competitors for your next promotion possess skills/experience you do not possess?	0	1

Did you reach final shortlist in your last job interview?	1	0
Could you identify the differentiating point between you and the selected person?	1	0
Are you overworking to find sufficient time for new skills development?	0	1
Have the job requirements for your next promotion changed in the past one year?	1	0
Have you identified gaps in your skill set for changing job requirements?	1	0
Do you have a PLP to acquire above skill set?	1	0

Scoring Method

Add A and B to get E (A + B = E)

Add C and D to get F (C + D = F)

Add E and F to get the final score, G (E + F = G [Final Score])

Score 30–40: Best of luck. Your knowledge and skills are at cutting edge. You are on the right path to attain your goals.

Score 20–30: You possess competencies and skills to be on top of your current job but need to work on the next set of skills for the future career plan.

Score 10–20: You require reflection and introspection to identify gaps in your competencies and skills. You have maximum one year to get on top of situation.

Score 0–10: You are on road for fast obsolescence of knowledge and skills. Urgently engage a mentor or coach to take you through reflection and introspection to identify gaps in your learning plan and take active steps to acquire competencies and skills.

About the Authors

Suhayl Abidi is the co-author of *The VUCA Company*. He is an MBA from Faculty of Management Studies (FMS), University of Delhi, and PG Diploma in Information Management from Leeds Polytechnic, UK. For 25 years, he has worked for organizations such as Penguin Publishing, the British Council, Saudi Ports Authority, Reliance Industries, Essar and Piramal Healthcare in the information and organization learning domain. He has been responsible for design, implementation and dissemination of processes by which knowledge is captured, shared and used. Abidi has successfully completed several projects such as on Intranet, continuous learning programmes, learning from corporate history, web-based digital corporate library, digital archives, performance management system, e-zines, etc. Later, he consulted for companies such as CRISIL Limited and Kohinoor Group. He conducts training programmes in areas of developing agility, adaptability and resilience through continuous learning. He has written a number of articles in leading business papers and magazines.

Manoj Joshi is the co-author of *The VUCA Company*. He is currently Professor of Entrepreneurship, Innovation and

Family Business Strategy at Amity Business School and Director of Centre for VUCA Studies, Amity University, Lucknow. He is a B. Tech., MBA, Chartered Engineer and a Fellow of Institution of Engineers (Mech.). He is the Regional Editor India, *Journal of Family Business Management* by Emerald; Regional Editor, *International Journal of Strategic Business Alliances* by Inderscience and editorial board member for international journals such as *Asia Pacific Journal of Management, Journal of Small Business Management, Business Strategy and Environment, Journal of Entrepreneurship in Emerging Economies, World Review of Entrepreneurship, Management and Sustainable Development,* etc. In the industry, he was associated with fluid engineering vertical, with expertise in design, manufacturing and business development. His current consulting includes VUCA strategy, entrepreneurship, innovation and family business from the behavioural perspective. He has travelled extensively and has over 26 years of combined experience in the areas of screw pumps design, heat exchangers, loading arms, projects, consulting, research, mentoring and teaching. He is an avid reader and enjoys cycling, trekking in Himalayas, with added interests in astronomy, astrophysics and watching movies with deep interests in life after death.